EGOPRENEUR

For Mieke.

This book was originally published as *Egopreneur. Ik zorg voor mezelf dus ik ben*, LannooCampus, 2019.

D/2020/45/95 – ISBN 978 94 014 6680 6 – NUR 740, 801

Cover and interior design: Gert Degrande | De Witlofcompagnie

© Paul Van Den Bosch & Lannoo Publishers nv, Tielt, 2020.

LannooCampus Publishers is a subsidiary of Lannoo Publishers,
the book and multimedia division of Lannoo Publishers nv.

LannooCampus Publishers
Vaartkom 41 box 01.02   P.O. Box 23202
3000 Leuven   1100 DS Amsterdam
Belgium   Netherlands

www.lannoocampus.com

PAUL VAN DEN BOSCH

EGO PRE NEUR

REACH THE TOP WITHOUT LOSING YOURSELF

LANNOO
CAMPUS

'Egopreneurs are entrepreneurs who devote a significant part of their efforts to self-improvement, to become more productive in their professional environment and to better support people in their immediate environment.'

Contents

Foreword

I began my career as a sports coach in 1988. My athletes expected me to improve their performance, to raise it to the next level. Ever faster, ever further, ever stronger. Sometimes it worked, sometimes it didn't. The difference between an athlete's heaven and hell was sometimes fractions of a second. But these fractions could make a world of difference. The result of training was often disappointing, even discouraging. Even if everything seemed to be under control and even though everything possible had been done, my athletes, and by extension myself, could still go home empty-handed.

For 30 years, I gave the best of myself to my athletes, but gradually a new dimension entered my professional life: the coaching of people outside of sport. I meet so many passionate and driven people who put everything into their work and their family, but nothing or at least not enough into themselves. This lack of self-concern and self-care often results in new struggles.

As with athletes, it is often the case that people outside of sport who are physically fit are also mentally resilient, and that people who are mentally strong are also physically strong and recover quickly. For this reason, the health aspect, with an emphasis on sufficient exercise, sleep and the right diet, is of the utmost importance to me as a coach. If people trust my advice and actually start to take better care of themselves, I soon see that they not only improve physically, but also mentally, and that as a result neither of us are left empty-handed. We are always rewarded with success. Therein lies the major difference between coaching sportsmen and women and coaching 'ordinary' people.

In this book I will describe my day-to-day activities, but I will also explain my philosophy of life that underpins my activities. I hope that this will help you to perform like an athlete. To become faster, better and more powerful in all fields and at all levels.

My special thanks go to my co-author, Ann Van Loock, who helped write this book and who gave constructive feedback, challenged me and opened my eyes to new ways of seeing. In short, she often passed me the ball, so that all I had to do was knock it into the goal. Without her, this book would not have been possible. The same warm thanks go also to Bart Schols, whose detailed advice and feedback made a huge contribution to the final text. Finally, my thanks also go to Veronica Luedke, who was invaluable in making this English version possible.

Introduction

One of the first people I coached outside of the sporting world was Hans[1]. Hans is a highly respected CEO of a company that today employs some 800 people. I first got to know him in April 2016. After only a few minutes, he confided in me: 'I am stuck in a rut, completely stuck'. During the conversation that followed, a number of things soon became clear. Hans was leading the transformation of his company. He had also spent considerable time and effort defining the new direction that his company would follow in the years ahead.

For Hans, keeping communication channels open to his colleagues was crucial, as was leading by example. A self-confessed communications maniac, he thought it was important that every e-mail should be answered by his team as quickly as possible, or at least within a reasonable time-frame. To set the right example, he felt obliged to personally read and reply to each of his many e-mails, every day. It meant he worked most days until late in the evening, often clocking up working weeks of 80 hours or more.

---

1   All the people who are mentioned by their real name in this book have given their prior permission.

Over time, this punishing schedule had taken a toll on him, both professionally and personally. When we first met, Hans still had roughly one year to serve of his second three-year mandate as CEO. He hoped that he would be able to complete that mandate, but he could not envision renewing his contract. He was becoming overwhelmed, like a tired runner struggling to the end of a very hard marathon. When I asked him what he wanted to achieve in his private life, he answered that he wanted to write a book. But that was impossible in his current circumstance. How could he ever write a book with such a time-consuming job?

Nowadays, people in all walks of life and at all levels of society feel stuck in a rut. Business leaders, teachers, professionals, people in commercial functions: for many, it has become, or is rapidly becoming, all too much. In 2016, more than 320 million doses of anti-depressants were taken in Belgium, an increase of 100 million doses than just 10 years ago. These are frightening statistics, but they are nothing new. As long ago as June 1983, the American magazine *Time* warned that stress was destined to become the biggest single cause of death by the 21st century. Slowly but surely, that prediction is coming true.

Eminent writers and thinkers like Hans Rosling (author of the book *Factfulness: Ten Reasons We're Wrong About the World – and Why Things Are Better Than You Think*) and Maarten Boudry (author of the book *Why the World Isn't Going to the Dogs*) have tried to show us in a reasoned and incontrovertible way that many aspects of today's world are improvements on the past. But I often feel that the Peter Principle best describes today's society: people in a hierarchy tend to rise to their level of incompetence. Our society has become so 'developed' that it is getting out of control and is increasingly unable to regulate itself adequately. The proof? You need to look no further than the problem of global warming and the yearly increase in burn-outs.

We have reached the point where one is justified to speak of societal derailment and there is no obvious solution to get us quickly back on track. The world has become too complex. Our ears are assailed each day by new and more disturbing prophecies of doom. Many people feel that the demands made on them are spiralling out of control. Their flexibility and resilience are being stretched further, and further and further, until they snap. No wonder, then, that countless men and women feel exhausted and can no longer see the light at the end of the tunnel, to the point that anti-depressants become their remedy of last resort.

ACHIEVING MORE WITH A LOWER SCORE

Despite these conditions, some people seem better able to deal with this complexity than others. Thankfully, not everyone suffers from burn-out and not everyone has a pessimistic view of the future. So, what is it that makes these people different?

Superficially, such people seem to have a thick skin. They appear to cope with complexity better than others. A closer look reveals that in the majority of cases they are men and women who resist being driven to distraction by the pursuit of perfection. They do not strive to achieve 100% success in all they do, having found that an 80% success rate is usually enough. Odd as It may seem, they have learned that being satisfied with less makes them more resilient and boosts their performance. Another important benefit of this approach is that it helps them free up more time for themselves, time that they can use for the things that are important and personally fulfilling.

To escape from his rut, Hans needed to change lots of things in his life. He had to learn even better how to delegate, how to make more time for himself and how to avoid focusing on non-urgent matters, so that he could concentrate on the bigger picture. At the same time, I also recognised that, as his coach, I needed to focus on another contributor to Hans' stress.

I am 100% convinced that there is a fundamental connection between a person's mental and physical status. I believe that good physical fitness enhances mental resilience and that great mental strength enhances physical recovery. For example, the successful Japanese author Haruki Murakami goes running for an hour each day. In his book *Novelist as a Vocation* he explains why: 'Physical and spiritual energy are like two wheels of the same cart. They work best when they are in balance, to keep you on the right path and to better develop your strength.' I could not agree more. That is why, for me, having a holistic approach to the people I coach is so important: I need to work on their body and their mind. You cannot help someone through a mental dip unless you devote equal attention to their mental and their physical condition. Hans' problems reflected this. He had shamefully neglected his physical state in recent years. He was overweight, took almost no daily exercise and had an average of only four to five hours of sleep each night. It was immediately clear to me that getting him to adopt a healthier lifestyle was the most important element of the coaching trajectory that I would map out for him.

DESCENDING TO CLIMB HIGHER

To explain the origins of my specific approach, I need to take you back in time. Between 1974 and 1978, I studied what was then called physical education (it is now sporting sciences) at Belgian university KU Leuven. I wanted to be a sports teacher and help young people to learn about the basic principles and practices of the most important sports.

The descent from Global Dynamic Coordination (GDC) is a powerful didactic method used to teach students the fundamental skills for any given sport, also called its global form. If a specific skill is not present, it is practised individually. This is referred to as a descent from GDC. Consider volleyball. If students lack sufficient skills for overhead passing of the ball, the game would be stopped and exercises to acquire or improve the hand skills would be performed. Once the lesson had been learned or the hand position corrected, the global game would restart. If a further weakness or error was noted, the GDC would stop again and a new descent initiated. Instruction would continue in this manner until the students had mastered all the techniques necessary to play the global game correctly.

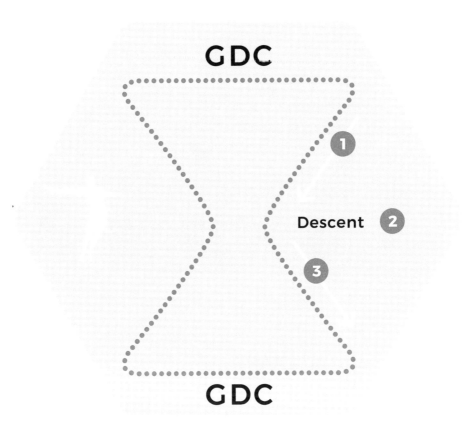

DESCENT FROM THE GLOBAL DYNAMIC COORDINATION

This method can also be used to prevent us from getting stuck in a rut or to get out of a rut we are in, so that we can gain better control over the totality of our lives. To apply this didactic system, we first need to change the starting point from GDC to GCW (Global Complex World). It is from this GCW that we should descend by performing exercises that help us in how we bear up under the complexity that surrounds us by making us stronger and more resilient, both mentally and physically. These descents force us to learn to take better care of ourselves, with the most important descent being the need to exercise more, eat healthier, and sleep better.

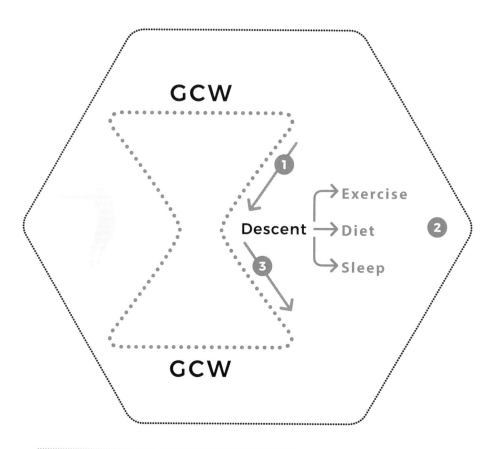

DESCENT FROM THE GLOBAL COMPLEX WORLD

BECOMING A STRONGER ME

This is precisely the method I used with Hans and with later coachees. It may sound simple, but it isn't. Just like mastering any complex athletic skill, you need to make several descents, and some descents will need to be repeated more than once. Automatisms are not necessarily instinctive so they sometimes must be learned. Sometimes you need to hit the same nail on the head repeatedly.

A common problem arises when coaching people towards a healthier lifestyle and greater mental resilience: they all have good reasons for remaining stuck in their complex world. This means that they fail to free up enough time to take proper care of themselves. Meetings, targets and other work pressures, the kid's homework, the kid's taxi service on weekends (art school, tennis lessons, etc.) and 101 other family obligations all take up time. So often, my clients make time for everyone but themselves. They ignore the familiar lesson we hear each time we board an aeroplane: in the event of an emergency, put on your own oxygen mask first, then help your children and your fellow passengers. Only when you have enough oxygen, can you be of help to others. This is a rule that applies in our everyday life, even down here on the ground.

Egopreneur is intended to help you to become a stronger and more resilient 'me', so that you can function better in an increasingly complex world, thereby allowing you to also take better care of others.

This book is written for everyone who is struggling to deal with too much pressure and too little time; for everyone who has the feeling that chasing the facts is the only form of exercise they get. *Egopreneur* is here to help you become a stronger, more resilient 'me', so that you can function better in an increasingly complex world, allowing you to also take better care of others.

In the first part of this book, you will find numerous insights that will help you make time for yourself, so that you can care for yourself adequately. The most important prerequisite for success is your willingness to accept that 80% is good enough in everything that you do. This will be a serious 'mind switch' for many. But remember that 80% should never be seen as setting the bar too low. Most of us would have been more than happy with 80% at school or university – which is still more than enough to get you a *cum laude* diploma!

The second part of this book provides an in-depth look at the connection between a healthy lifestyle and high stress-resistance, and it offers concrete tips on how to exercise more, eat (and drink) better, and sleep more soundly. These little pieces of advice are both useful and, more importantly, achievable, provided you first understand the 'why'. For this reason part one will focus heavily on these 'why' questions, so you know exactly how to apply these tips in part two.

> In the meantime, things are going well for Hans. His lifestyle has undergone a complete makeover. He has lost weight, improved his sleep patterns and now, three years later, manages an average of 9000 steps per day. He applied for a third term as his company's CEO and was awarded a new three-year mandate by the board of directors. He has also realised his dream of publishing a book. Not to mention, the people around him are happy. And in Hans, I have acquired a new and very dear friend for life.

PART 1

EGO
PRE
NEUR

1

When 100% is too much

When another one of my clients, cyclo-cross rider Sven Nys, retired from competition, lots of people asked me how I would 'fill my days' – and I was always amazed. Apparently, everyone thought that most of my available time went into coaching Sven. This was most certainly not the case.

Input and output

Have you ever noticed that your input and output are not always distributed evenly? On one occasion you can accomplish a lot in a short time with seemingly little effort, while on other occasions you can put your heart and soul into a project but it never really seems to get you far.

This same observation can be made in many other fields. In the corporate world, for example, 20% of a company's products are responsible for 80% of its turnover (if things are going well). In the world of books, 20% of authors are responsible for 80% of sales. And as far as the world's wealth is concerned, 80% of it is in the hands of the richest 20% of the population.

This recurring phenomenon, known as the law of unequal distribution, or more popularly the 80/20% principle (which I'll refer to as 80/20 or 20/80), was first described by the Italian economist Vilfredo Pareto (1843). He recognised that cause and effect are seldom in balance and that sometimes there can be huge discrepancies between input and output. In most cases, a small part of the input (or effort) leads to the biggest part of the output (or result).

Simply put: as a general rule, just 20% of your effort achieves a whopping 80% of your result. This means, of course, that to achieve the remaining 20% of your result you need to expend 80% of your effort (energy, time, etc.). In other words, for this final 20% of your result, the input is much greater than the output.

A small effort
can achieve a
great result.

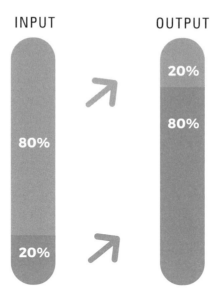

PARETO'S 80/20 PRINCIPLE

Since Pareto first formulated it, this principle has been reinvented time and time again and used in almost every imaginable domain. Of course, the 80/20 proportionality does not always apply. Sometimes an even smaller input can result in an even greater output. For example, just 1% of all existing words are used 80% of the time, and 1% of all the world's people own more than 50% of the entire world's wealth.

TRAINING HARDER FOR INCREASINGLY LESS RETURN

The Pareto principle can also be found in the world of sport. Here, it is linked to another principle, notably, the law of diminishing returns. The diagram on the next page clarifies this idea. If your level of fitness is very low and you start to train, initially you will make significant progress in a relatively short period of time. But as your physical condition improves, it will become increasingly difficult to further improve your performance. In fact, you will need to train longer, harder and with more sophisticated methods to achieve only minimal improvement.

Everyone is free to follow this particular path if they choose. Everyone, that is, except top athletes. They have no choice. They must do everything they can to achieve every possible improvement. In this sense, elite sport is a daily battle against the law of diminishing returns.

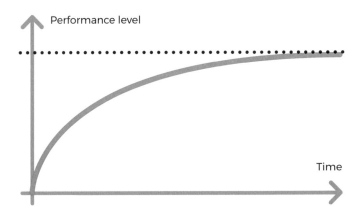

THE PRINCIPLE OF DIMINISHING RETURNS

Things are different for recreational athletes. Let's take the example of a typical recreational cyclist riding 5000 - 6000 kilometres per year. If he trains wisely, a more than acceptable level of performance is achievable. Of course, his results will also depend on talent.

Now, let's imagine that our cyclist wants to increase his level of performance and decides to boost his mileage to 10 000 kilometres per year. 5000 extra kilometres, at an average speed of 28 kilometres per hour, equates to about 178 hours extra in the saddle over the course of a year. The equivalent of four working weeks! The cyclist will invest much more of his time in his hobby, but what will this extra effort bring in terms of improvement, and will it be worth it?

This is an important decision for all recreational athletes. Do we push ourselves to our personal limits to capture every possible last gram, millimetre or second of performance regardless of the time it takes? Perhaps. But it's important to realise that our initial efforts yield the greatest return and that overinvesting energy in sport will rob us of the energy needed for other aspects of life. The amount of energy at our disposal is (sadly) not limitless. It's true that exercise also brings energy – but only up to a point. Let's look at it later in more detail.

The take-home message: is it worth expending so much extra energy on something that offers marginal return? In other words, is it worth spending 80% of your time and energy to achieve a 20% increase (or even less) in result? Or is it smarter to give the Pareto principle a try, and keep some energy in reserve?

What is your preferred level of input?

We can classify people into three groups using the Pareto principle. I call them the 20/80er, the 80/20er and the 100%er. In the first two categories, the first figure represents the initial input and the second figure represents the output. In other words, the 20/80er uses 20% of their time or energy to achieve 80% of the result, while the 80/20er uses 80% of their time or energy to achieve just 20% of the result (wasting/losing a lot of time and/or energy). The 100%er always applies 100% of their available time and energy to every task in the hope of achieving the best possible result. The 100%ers are perfectionists. They work to the highest level of detail and are constantly looking for ways to improve.

So who do you want to be?

100%ER: TOP OF THE CLASS.
(FOR NOW)

There will always be people who 'shoot for the moon': 100% flat out, all the time. Top athletes, for example, have no choice. If they want to succeed, they have to give everything they have and focus exclusively on just one thing: their athletic discipline. Nothing else matters. That extra centimetre, a tenth of a second, a higher ranking – all of these things make the difference between second place and the top rung of the athletic ladder. These athletes are prepared to sacrifice everything to achieve their ultimate goal.

In recent years, the concept of 'marginal gains' has found its way into elite athletics, largely under the influence of the new approach adopted by the British cycling team: Team Sky (now Team INEOS). There comes a point when the physical and mental limit of a top athlete has been reached, so that further progression can't be made by simply training. The only way to further enhance performance is to study all the factors that contribute to performance in minute detail, including equipment, diet, food supplements, patterns of sleep, etc. Improvements in these factors can lead to marginal gains.

This may sound nice, but it is important to remember that an athlete will only achieve maximum return through correct application of the basics, training with a focus on the balance of effort and recovery. Too many of today's coaches lose sight of this. They are so busy searching for marginal gains that they neglect the physical and mental foundation where significant progress in performance can often still be made.

I've worked with many top athletes throughout my career. The higher they climbed up the athletic ladder of success, the more they dedicated themselves completely to their disciplines. They succeeded in building a whole team around them (manager, personal coach, scientists, technicians, financial adviser, team mates, etc.), so that their 'task' was reduced to an exclusive focus on two essentials: training and performance. This explains why top athletes are often thought of as egocentric. Almost by definition, they stand at the centre of their own universe.

> Too many people lose sight
> of their limits, so that they
> almost systematically go
> beyond those limits.

The ideal of the elite athlete is not exclusive to the world of professional sport. Sometimes I am approached by recreational athletes who are also fanatically focused on their favourite sport and all that it involves, such as diet and equipment. Some of them want the same honed physical perfection of a trained professional athlete with a super-low-fat body mass and they are prepared to do almost anything to achieve it. But why? Just like a real top athlete, they run the risk that their fanaticism will undo them: by pushing their body too far, too often, they will actually perform worse!

It can be very difficult to make these recreational fanatics understand that a less extreme approach to their hobby will lead to better results. Like a racehorse, most of them are wearing blinkers. For them, there is only one objective and one way to achieve it – and they do whatever it takes to turn their dream into reality. But like the blinkered racehorse, 100% focus can lead to tunnel vision or loss of the wider perspective. Yet often, they just don't care. They are perfectionists, so perfection is the only option.

Does this mean that perfectionism by definition is always wrong? No. We all have times when we have to give it everything we have, when only the best will do. But you shouldn't overdo it. You can't strive to be perfect all the time. Today, I meet far too many people who lose sight of their limits, and almost systematically go beyond those limits. After a while, even 100% effort is no longer enough: it needs to be 120%!

It is the same in the business world. Today, many people – far too many people – are getting up earlier and earlier each morning to check their e-mails, prepare for meetings, etc. And when they return home, they end up working on their laptops for a few more hours until it is time to go to bed. Of course, this often means having trouble getting up the next morning, so that they miss morning breakfast with the family and set off into the rush hour only half-washed and with an empty stomach! These people, who always seem to be struggling to catch up, are suffering from the business variant of FOMO: fear of missing out. And I don't mean fear of missing out on the good things in life. No, it is fear of missing something that might be crucial for their career.

Inevitably, these people become 120/80ers: with their huge input, their return fails to grow. And then the opposite happens. With time, they score no better than 20/80ers and even risk losing out completely, not only in terms of return, but also in their general quality of life. Is it any wonder that the number of people suffering from burn-out is increasing at alarming rates every day?

THE 80/20ER

Some people expend – again, sometimes without a choice – 80% of their time and energy to achieve a tangible return of just 20% or even less. Countless people today feel that their work produces no measurable added value for their employer and that, consequently, they simply tread water. They spend a lot of time on tasks with little perceived impact, so they end up feeling worthless and even 'overpaid' for the work that they do.

Unsurprisingly, this syndrome leads to a lack of satisfaction and a general feeling of frustration. They begin to feel unhappy at work. It's perfectly understandable: who wouldn't feel frustrated to achieve so little gain for so much effort?

The next stage in this negative downwards spiral is often extreme boredom, and if it persists the spectre of bored-out is just around the corner. Bored-out is the opposite of burned-out but is no less serious. Bored-out people have trouble facing and accepting new challenges.

Of course, there are always people who simply waste their time, either because they can't focus, because they occupy themselves with too many unimportant things simultaneously, or because they're 'distracted' by e-mails, office small-talk, social media, etc. They are 'busy' all day, but actually achieve very few positive results.

THE 20/80ER

I hope that you now understand why the 20/80 option is the most obvious and also the most effective way to allocate time and energy. Or at least it should be. As a 20/80er, you achieve with your best 20% of the effort no less than 80% of the maximum possible return. Perhaps you think that aiming for an 80% return is not ambitious enough? If so, remember what was said in the introduction: at university, 80% is enough to get you a *cum laude* degree, something achieved by very few people. So, what's wrong with aiming for 80% in your professional life?

Setting 80% as your goal removes the pressure associated with 'having' to achieve 100%, which all too often leads to frustration and tunnel vision. Additionally, it allows you to free up time for other projects, because 80% of your time and energy remains unused!

Theoretically, this means that you could deal with four projects instead of just one and that you should be able to achieve an 80% return from each of them. This means that you could focus on multiple topics simultaneously with a possibility of these projects complementing one another.

Bart, one of my coachees, needed to stay abreast of the daily news to carry out his work. As a result, he spent two or three hours each morning reading various newspapers from cover to cover, then drove to his office to begin the hectic preparations for his news and current affairs programme on national television.

In time, it became clear to Bart that just reading the headlines and cursorily scanning the most important articles was more than enough to find out what he needed to know. His editorial team did the rest. Once the subjects for that evening's programme had been chosen, Bart studied them thoroughly and then… he suddenly discovered that he had time left over for himself. As a result, he started doing some sport, which made him fitter and more resilient than he already was.

Teaching is one of many professions suffering from 'planning-itis'. Teachers are overwhelmed with paperwork, leaving them with increasingly less time to focus on the most essential aspect of their work: giving lessons and teaching children. Some would argue that there are good reasons for an emphasis on planning, but there is no denying that for many teachers it's a burden. But does it need to be? Is there no way around it? Perhaps there is.

Each teacher deals with tedious administrative formalities in their own way. Some are able to distance themselves to some extent from planning, allowing them to free up time for the most important tasks. For example, a language teacher might find time to help with the local drama group's upcoming production, or maybe open reading club, or even take up training on new teaching methods. These different activities cross-fertilise, creating new energy that can help keep bored-out and burned-out at bay.

Teachers like this focus on their schools and on their pupils' objectives 'at all costs' and still manage to broaden the horizons of their students. The quality of their lessons, and the likelihood that their pupils will reach their targets, increase. An absolute precondition for this is – contradictory to current practice – regional educational authorities and the governing bodies of individual schools subscribing to this enlightened vision. They must accept that further administrative burdens (for example, preparation for a school review) can only be to the detriment of the school, its teachers and its pupils.

Some teachers are able to put excessive administrative tasks in due perspective allowing them to concentrate more fully on their core tasks. Yet, the majority of teachers are overwhelmed and find it difficult adapting to feeling like a single gear in a large machine or a single link in a long chain.

TOP WORK

Let's be clear on one thing. The case above is not an argument or an excuse for low quality work or for making mistakes. Your 20% effort should be performed to the necessary standard of excellence. A doctor cannot allow himself to write a wrong prescription or make a bad diagnosis. A driver who only abides by 20% of the rules of the road would be a danger to us all. Technicians who maintain planes between flights need to check all the crucial parts.

Work must always be carried out efficiently and effectively, but you can't do it alone. You need to surround yourself with the right people who, together with you, ensure that 100% of what needs to be done actually gets done, and gets done properly. This is the key to being multifunctional and to performing successfully at the highest level.

YOUR MOST IMPORTANT 20%

Until now, I have only spoken about the four projects you can undertake, each of which require 20% of your time and achieve an 80% in return. 20% of your time remains unused – and this is perhaps the most interesting 20%.

I strongly advise using this 20% for self-improvement, to develop and care for yourself. Invest this 20% in a company called YOU. Become a kind of self-entrepreneur, a manager of your own well-being and the things that can contribute towards it. We are all in charge of a small but very important SME: our own body and mind. Do we not owe it to ourselves to take responsibility for our *company* and all its assets – to take good care of who and what we are?

A 20/80er keeps some
time for himself.

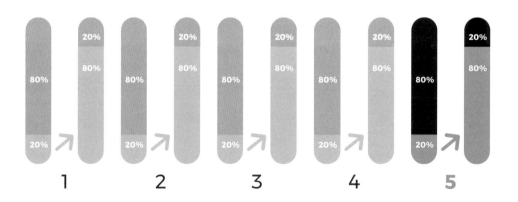

1   2   3   4   5

TIME FOR A FIFTH PROJECT: TIME FOR YOURSELF

To be a successful 20/80er, you need to always find the best focus for your 20% effort. Remember, if you need to invest only 20% of your energy in one project to get the best results, then you're free to invest in five projects. Don't overlook the need to keep the last and most important 20% for a special purpose: you.

THAT IS HOW YOU BECOME AN EGOPRENEUR.

Back to the subject of Sven Nys' retirement from competitive sport. Since 1988, I worked with a number of top athletes, one for 16 years, another for 14 years and with Sven for 13 years. In some cases, I was the only coach an athlete had in their careers. My athletes knew that I was there for them, unconditionally. They could count on me day or night.

In addition to my life as a coach, I've had other responsibilities and interests. For 38 years I taught (much of it part-time). In 2009 I founded the Energy Lab training guidance centre with Bob Verbeeck (CEO of the Golazo sport marketing company) and have since helped it become the fantastic company it is today, with more than 40 super-enthusiastic colleagues.

I remain closely involved with the Energy Lab and continue to coach top athletes and also people outside of athletics. I give dozens of lectures each year and occasionally write books like the one you're reading now. All of this because I see the importance of taking care of myself. I'm a regular cyclist and runner, and devote sufficient time to my family and friends.

In other words, even when I was coaching Sven Nys, I had a lot of time left over. I always did what I had to do for him, but I also focused on the most important 20%. I made up a detailed weekly training schedule and personally ensured that it was correctly implemented every single day. I was his sounding board and mental coach. I went to his winter races. And no matter when, I was available. But there were many other time-consuming things that I didn't do. I never sat on the motorbike in front of him when he had to do motorpacing sessions. I never accompanied him on training trips to Mallorca. I was never at his road races. I never had anything to do with his bikes and equipment.

Other people contributed to areas outside of my specialisation. They filled the remaining 80% that I wasn't involved in. Together we gave the 100% of what Sven needed, leaving him to focus 100% (and with great success) on his career. This is how I made time for other athletes amidst other initiatives.

THIS WAS POSSIBLE
BECAUSE I'M A 20/80ER.
I AM AN **EGOPRENEUR**.

Question round

» Is your input proportionate to your output?

» How much satisfaction does your work give you?

» To what extent do you feel empathy for the 20/80er?

2

The right

way

> The motto of my college is engraved over the lectern in the study room. It is old and worn but clearly visible: *Ick pooghe om d'hooge* ('I try to climb higher'). I looked at it each evening while I studied. It was only much later that I understood that this is another way of saying: *'Plus est en vous' or* 'there is more in you than you think', a well-known saying of the Jesuits.

From an early age and across the course of our lives we are pushed 'to do things well' or 'to do our best'. Parents like to have perfect children who are perfectly prepared for adulthood. Children pick up on this and express their 'perfect as possible' lives on social platforms like Facebook and Instagram. But there are many reasons for <u>not</u> seeking perfection – for being satisfied with 80% based on your strongest 20%, for being a 20/80er – an Egopreneur.

Focus on your strengths

As a coach, I quickly understood that my athletes could only excel when they made best use of their strengths. And by further developing these strengths wherever possible. My goal is to turn a good sprinter into a better sprinter and a good climber into a better climber.

One of the cyclists I coach, Thomas De Gendt, has rightly been 'crowned' the king of the long breakaway. He has a unique ability to escape from the peloton early on in a race, taking with him a limited number of other riders. He's equally unmatched in his ability to keep ahead of the chasing peloton, sometimes over distances in excess of 100 kilometres, and bring his breakaway to a winning conclusion. This manner of cycling is his strong point and, for this reason precisely, the volume and intensity of his training is geared to reflect it. This involves training to give him even more substance, to enable him to maintain the same unbroken high tempo for even longer periods.

Tinkering with weakness in an effort to improve it is usually a waste of time and achieves little or nothing. This doesn't mean that we shouldn't be on the lookout for hidden talents. We need to recognise real talent – and focus on them.

Regrettably we live in a culture that prefers to focus on the things that go wrong, so that much real talent is lost or stays undetected.

For example, teachers and parents have a tendency to concentrate on the subjects with poor or below average results when reading their children's school reports. In this way, they often overlook the good results elsewhere in the same report!

Likewise, parent-teacher evenings at school get all too often bogged down by hammering on the same weak points. Instead, teachers, pupils and parents should together, and through discussion, try to paint a more complete picture. And do this not by focusing solely on the one 'not good enough' mark, but by emphasising the '90%' on the pupil's best subject. It should be cherished, by pupils _and_ parents alike. Cherished and further stimulated. Frequently, these teacher-pupil-parent discussions end with a single (wrong) question: how can that not good enough be eliminated?

This reflex is embedded in our system. But the energy devoted to it often affects the student's performance and where the student once excelled, they begin to stagnate rather than further improve. It's a pity, because the pleasure the pupil experiences in his/her favourite subjects will decline proportionally. And by the time the next parent-teacher evening comes around, there's another 'not good enough' that needs to be addressed and remedied.

> ## Do not focus compulsively
> ## on weak points.
> ## You make the difference
> ## with your strengths.

This argument isn't in favour of doing nothing about the 'not good enough' so that it becomes even worse. It's an argument against focusing compulsively on a weak point. Every pupil _and_ teacher must learn how to implement effective damage control. This damage must be kept within reasonable bounds, so that the pupil retains energy and enthusiasm for their favourite subjects, scores well, and is awarded a diploma. It's much better than implementing a strategy to generate average scores that frequently reflect a pupil's disinterested approach to learning.

In the context of cycling, this is not to suggest that a sprinter's coach shouldn't attempt to make their clients better climbers if, for example, they are taking part in hard mountain stages like in the Tour de France. The aim must be to help the sprinter to survive the mountain stages by beating the time limit, so that they stay in the race and can make best use of their strengths in the sprint finish stages. But you shouldn't overdo it or forget the more important positive points. As a teacher or a coach, you should not demonstrate your intention to help your pupil or athlete by constantly focusing on their weak points.

In all walks of life, in sports, academics or professional life, it is important to play to your strengths. This is the only way that you will ever be able to excel. Excellence is achieved on the basis of maximising your strengths, not on the improvement of your weaknesses. It is the 10 out of 10s that make the difference.

In an interview in the Flemish *De Tijd* newspaper in January 2019, Patrick De Maeseneire, ex-CEO of the international Adecco employment agency, described his participation in a training course at Apple. During the first week, the focus was on identifying his strengths and weaknesses, so that during the second and subsequent weeks these weaknesses could be turned into strengths, allowing him to be some kind of entrepreneurial superman. After six weeks, he felt totally confused and frustrated, because he was no longer able to concentrate on what he was good at. Since then, he returned to focusing on his strong points and surrounding himself with people who can make up for his weaknesses.

My experience as a coach has allowed me to see that this phenomenon of strengths versus weakness is a widespread problem. After giving a lecture on the qualities of coaching leadership, I was approached by the branch manager of a bank who had an urgent problem with one of his employees. When this person was hired he seemed to have all the right qualifications and skills and was expected to have a promising career with the bank. Unfortunately, it soon became clear that he was not performing well in his job as a teller. He was clumsy with customers and some of them had complained about his perceived incompetence. He was simply not able to convince people of his qualities (which he undoubtedly possessed) as a competent bank clerk. The manager asked me if I thought it was a good idea to send the employee on a course to improve his communication skills, so that he could interact more effectively with the bank's clients.

By now, I understood that the manager had not understood one of the essential points I had made in my lecture – why focus exclusively on the employee's weak point (people management) and ignore his other positive qualities? Focusing on the employee's weaknesses might result in some improvements but never enough.

My advice to the manager was simple: to find another job for the man that would allow him to use the talents in which he could excel and to put someone else on the front desk who was better equipped to deal with customers. This would benefit both the bank and the man himself!

CONCLUSION: FOCUS ON DEVELOPING **TALENTS** MORE THAN ON OVERCOMING WEAKNESSES.

Say 'no' in good time!

The customer, they say, is always right. But perhaps not always. Everyone who has ever had to deal with customers knows that they can sometimes be very demanding, so that the corresponding workload for staff becomes too much to manage. For this reason, it's important to agree on ground rules for customer interactions, and on a strategy to educate customers. There is no point in trying to give the customer everything they want at any cost.

It is tempting to say yes to every proposition. I've had to say no several times to athletes who were searching for a new coach, because I knew that I would be taking on too much or because the athlete's expectations were too high, making our collaboration likely to end in mutual frustration. For example, if an athlete asks me to make him a world champion, I always refuse. Those are ambitions that I can never hope to fulfil.

Above all, never say yes simply because you want to please someone. The British pop idol Ed Sheeran expressed it cogently in a 2011 tweet: 'I can't tell you the key to success but the key to failure is trying to please everyone.' Trying to please everyone only ensures that your own vision of how things should be is increasingly pushed to one side or is even forgotten completely, and all to the benefit of others. What would this say about your own self-esteem? And how could you ever hope to keep up the pace on a treadmill that keeps getting faster and faster?

One of the reasons we say yes too often is to avoid or reduce conflict. It's something we've been brought up to see as a good thing. Another reason is that in life you're never certain of when opportunities are going to arise, so it may seem logical to seize every opportunity with enthusiasm. But we quickly realise that all the things we've said yes to will gradually mount to something unmanageable. Sooner or later always saying yes will lead to a crisis in your agenda, and in your life.

If you follow the 20/80 principle, and focus on the 20% that will bring you the best return, you will notice that it becomes easier to be more selective in handling propositions. You will know better when to say yes and, above all, no.

A good test is to look critically at your own agenda. Put a tick-mark beside the activities that you're genuinely passionate about. But what about all the other activities? Why are they causing doubt? Perhaps because you only said yes to please someone. Or because your gut feeling from the get-go was that it wasn't something you should've accepted. Or because it was something that didn't play to your strengths. Or because it would take up too much time. Or because, this way, you'll soon have a long list of activities that you see would have been better to say no to. Saying no becomes easier when you realise that there are so many other things that you can do with the precious 20% that you are interested in.

Be careful to avoid the danger of analysis for analysis' sake. If you fall into this trap, you will quickly find yourself suffering from analysis paralysis, so that you'll end up making no decisions at all. So analyse, but don't overdo it. And then decide! Reflect by all means, but don't ignore your gut feeling. Above all, always retain control over your own treadmill!

The golden rule: don't try to be perfect

When you adopt the 20/80 philosophy, you will immediately notice that your yearning for perfection disappears. You'll see that you're not a top athlete who needs to concentrate exclusively on a single activity, in which you must be the best. As a result, you understand that you need to take a step back from the perfectionist thinking that has so far dominated your entire life.

In today's world, you are too often expected to be a top performer in both your professional and private life. In addition to a busy job, you're expected to have interesting hobbies, to be able to face intense sporting challenges that allow you to explore your physical limits, either individually or with your friends. And while you're attempting to keep all these balls successfully in the air, you also have to prove these abilities through photos on Instagram or Facebook so that everyone can see how perfect you are. And others (those less fortunate in that particular respect) can see how they should take a page out of your book.

At first glance, it might seem that the aim of social media in our society is to promote openness and social contact, but too often it's used as a show of who's 'happiest' and 'most perfect'. It's a trap that many people still find hard to avoid.

The desire to be perfect can quickly push you into a downwards spiral that eats up your energy. In contrast, the 20/80 approach makes you aware of the need to deal sparingly with the energy available to you on any given day. Why waste time and effort on things that cannot contribute to your 20/80? Just to try and prove to everyone that you are good at everything? That is impossible. Be selective. Realising that there is no such thing as perfection in this world is the key to success.

Seek variety in your life

The philosopher Karl Marx introduced the concept that variety in work adds value. Writing at the end of the 19th century, during a period of rapidly increasing industrialisation, he saw how factory workers were exploited like gears in a gigantic machine without ever seeing the end product of their labour or being able to benefit from the huge wealth that capitalism generated.

Marx argued that it is only through seeing the end result that people are able to find the motivation to continue functioning as a gear, avoiding alienation. It's only then that they can realise that they are contributing towards a whole and that their contribution is essential. According to Marx, however, it was also necessary to take things a step further. He believed that it was not only important for workers to see the end product, but equally for them to have variation in their daily tasks. Repetitive tasks lead to mind-numbing mental sterility no matter how fascinating that work might be at the beginning.

In other words, variety is the key. 20/80 automatically gives variation to your life. As a 20/80er, you have the time and luxury to focus on different things. What's more, you're able to approach each of these with a fresh and open mind, without any feelings of monotony or boredom. The free time that being a 20/80er affords you will lead to numerous equally interesting activities. These will be projects that you have chosen consciously whilst saying 'no' to those projects that don't suit you. Marx's theory is perfectly suited to the 20/80 approach: variation as a fundamental principle.

Having time for everything

'Busy' is unquestionably the most used word of our generation. No-one seems to have time for anything and we all seem to be chasing our tails in circles. We're constantly saying: 'I don't know if I have time for that.' Whereas we should be saying: 'I don't know if I want to make the time for that.'

Being busy has become a status symbol in our western society. Some scientists have even promoted the vision that people should or must be busy. For example, Jordan Peterson, a leading and controversial intellectual and author of the bestseller *Twelve Rules for Life,* argues that people in the western world are not doing enough to try and live life 100% to the full. A survey carried out amongst his students revealed, according to Peterson, some worrying findings. He noted from their daily summaries of activities that some of them are wasting between four and six hours a day. As a result, he concluded: 'We are probably running at about 51% of our capacity.' Peterson estimates that these lacklustre students are 'losing' about 25 hours each week. That is equivalent to a hundred hours each month, multiplied by 50 dollars, etc. It adds up to a huge amount of time wasted on watching YouTube films, updating social media accounts, ineffective methods of study, etc. What these young people should be doing, says Peterson, is trying to get more out of their lives by performing better. But is that actually the case? Are we really flittering away our precious time? And would we truly be better off trying to achieve 100% in everything we do?

Being busy as a status symbol is a relatively new phenomenon. In his book *The Theory of the Leisure Class* (1899), the American economist Thorstein Veblen described how at the end of the 19th century ostentatious consumption and the pursuit of leisure activities were used to confirm or even enhance one's status. In other words, it was by <u>not</u> being constantly busy that you were able to improve your social standing! This was also the case in the Middle Ages, when vassals and serfs were expected to do all the hard work on your behalf. If we go back even further, to the time of the Romans and the Greeks, it was the same, slaves laboured night and day, while their masters sat back and enjoyed life.

So, to what extent should we believe claims about the efficiency and effectiveness of 'busy-busy-busy'? With my coachees I make the following comparison. As every gardening expert will tell you, every so often it's necessary to aerate your lawn. Well, it's precisely the same with your life and your thoughts: you sometimes need to give them a little space and air. Taking an occasional 'time-out' will allow you to grow better again in the future.

Of course, this applies equally to students. They can't be expected to work hard all the time. Every now and then they need to take a break, to get a breath of fresh air, do a little sport, and put their mind temporarily in first gear. It's the same for athletes: if they fail to stick to a training programme that allows sufficient aeration, they will end up running into a brick wall. Only then, often when it is too late, will they realise that they have been on the wrong track.

In her book *Pourquoi les Chinois ont-ils de temps* (*Why the Chinese Have Time to Spare*), the French philosopher Christine Cayol offers a vision of time and how we should use it that is very different from the perception we have in the western world. Time in China, she says, is not (as it's often the case in the West) like an arrow on its way to a target or like sand running out of an hourglass. For the Chinese, time is like water: something that sometimes swallows us, but something that can also buoy us, helping us to float. Having time is a status symbol in the new China. If, for example, you use 'busy-busy-busy' as an excuse for being late for an appointment in China, it's simply seen as a sign that you are doing things wrong. You should arrive early for your appointment, so that you can show that you have your life under control. By looking at time in this way, you create time for yourself. This is the time that we need for our remaining, and potentially most relevant, 20%.

Let's stay for a moment in the East and have a look at another country with a fascinating culture: Japan. The Japanese have a tradition of working hard over long and often unbroken periods of time. In extreme cases, this can lead to death by overworking, termed *karoshi*. This became a government acknowledged health risk in 1969 following the stroke-related death of a 29-year-old employee at one of Japan's leading newspapers. The Japanese government has attempted to combat this problem by promoting working from home and providing compensation for cases involving *karoshi*.

Conversely, Japan has a word for nothingness or negative space: 'Ma'. The Japanese concept of Ma is the pure and fundamental separation of things (by a void, space, hole, gulf, interval, gap, pause, etc.). Ma is the emptiness of possibilities, like a promise to be fulfilled. A particular space may seem cluttered, not because it contains too many things, but because there is too little space, not enough Ma between those things. Ma is also the time between successive notes in a piece of music or the space between words in a speech. These separations have the effect of strengthening the individual components. Indeed, it is Ma that makes minimalism possible. You can see Ma in art, in interior design, and in other instances where no single element dominates. Think, for example, of a typical Japanese home where a table and a few mats on the floor are the only decoration. The same perspective can also be applied to spiritual matters and can have a positive effect on everyday life.

Time and emptiness are not hollow concepts.

We need to focus more on these things in western society. Asian concepts of time and emptiness can be integrated into our lives and, in particular, into the 20% of our time that we guard for ourselves. Sometimes a little distance, time and space – in other words, some nothingness – can help us to deal effectively with the most important things in our lives.

Responding and adapting to a chaotic world

In our parents' and grandparents' day, it seemed as if life was lived according to a fixed pattern. You studied, gained qualifications, found a job, married and then started a family. Life moved more or less in a straight line, from school to retirement, from cradle to grave. This way of living has now almost completely disappeared. The relationships that shape our lives are no longer linear. People no longer keep the same job throughout their career. The world has become less predictable, its interactions more variable.

Nowadays, it is impossible to explain the world in terms of a single immutable law, as was the case with Newton's law of gravity. Think, for example, to the modern metaphor of how the beating of a butterfly's wings in China can cause a storm in America. It is increasingly difficult to identify and hold on to fixed patterns in the complex and chaotic world of today.

Perhaps we shouldn't see this constant changing as something negative or problematic, but rather as an opportunity to make our lives more interesting and more challenging. After all, there is much to be said for variation. Few would want their life to be wholly predictable.

This is where our 20/80 approach transforms us into an Egopreneur. Unpredictability offers us possibilities to evolve, to integrate new things into our lives in response to the chaotic world's increasing demands on our time. 20/80ers don't get bogged down giving 100% to a single activity that might even become obsolete. What would happen in the face of obsolescence? Would we find ourselves at sea, powerless to adapt? Or would we make use of the 20/80 principle and adjust our activities so that they once again become meaningful and relevant?

Does the flood of information at our finger tips make the world more predictable? Surely that's the intention of collecting massive amounts of data, so that everything can be neatly mapped out. In this way, we'll soon be able to gain control over everything, won't we?

Ironically, the opposite seems to be happening. Countless attempts have been made to make the world a more predictable place, but they remain just that: attempts. Yet, the world continues to be ever more chaotic. Given this situation, is it not vital to keep our options open, and poised to adapt where necessary? This is something you can only do as a 20/80er. Why? Let me tell you.

Why is it smart to embrace and cherish 20/80?

BECAUSE 20/80 PROMPTS YOU INTO ACTION

By not concentrating exclusively on a single project, you create new possibilities for yourself. Your environments stimulate the trial of new things, to fill in and adjust to your 4x20%. In other words, 20/80 prompts you to take action. It prevents you from entering a rut and missing out on opportunities for development. People who adopt 20/80 are not paralysed when a particular activity in their life disappears, because they are already familiar with many others that can take its place. 20/80ers never experience the metaphorical 'black hole' and are never troubled by the inertia that can occur when all your energy is focused on one thing.

BECAUSE YOU FEEL LESS STRESSED

As a 20/80er, you are able to make time for yourself, to have more than one purpose in your life. As a result, you're not subject to the stress that inevitably arises when you focus everything on a single activity. This gives you more time and opportunity to let go of things.

During my many years working with top performers, both inside and outside of sport, I have noticed that one of their most important qualities is their ability to continually look ahead to the future. Of course, they take the time to reflect on their most famous victories and defeats, but they're always keen to move forward again as quickly as possible. They don't waste energy finding excuses for why things failed, or building what if scenarios. They draw the right conclusions from what's happened and then let go of the past, ready to move on to the next challenge. They know that there's still so much to do, but not before they've paused to enjoy the moment. It's not easy, but it's oh so important. A 20/80 mind-set reduces stress.

BECAUSE YOU HAVE THE TIME TO DOUBT

Most people see doubt as something negative, as something to avoid. Yet in reality, having the courage to dare and to doubt is crucial for success. For example, the French philosopher Descartes systematically doubted everything, seeing it as the sole way to arrive at the truth.

By consistently investigating your doubts, you finally discover the things in your life that are necessary and true. Instead of ignoring these doubts and rushing ahead regardless, it pays to give them the time and attention they deserve, so that you can perhaps opt for a new and different 20%, one to which you can commit yourself fully.

It's sometimes necessary to use the Socratic Method (relation to the maieutic method) to raise questions and doubts alike, in either yourself or your coachee. Think of it as a prelude to acquiring novel and deeper insights: the coach acting as a kind of midwife for new ideas. Everyone can benefit from a process of critical self-examination, through which doubt can lead to positive renewal.

BECAUSE YOU MAKE TIME FOR YOURSELF AND …

Apply the tips that I will give in part two.

Key questions

» Do you make time for yourself?

» Do you focus on your strengths?

» Do you have too much junk in your life?

3

The
search

I have frequently received requests from talented and well-known athletes to be their coach. But no matter how brilliant their reputation, I've never given an immediate response. I've always taken a few days to think things through.

The theory outlined in the previous chapter sounds great, but how do you actually implement it in concrete terms in your day-to-day life? How can you ensure that you invest the right 20% into a given project? The following touchstones can help you in your search, but bear in mind that this will be a never-ending search. Your 20% is never definitive. You may think that's a pity. I think it is a blessing. The world around us is changing constantly. Nothing is static. That means in the long run your 20% will also change and continue changing. If this weren't the case, you'd soon find yourself out of date and left behind.

Reading to learn and to let go

To help you in your search for your right path, I think it's a good idea to keep on reading books that can shed light on possible best content for your 20%. Reading can help you to identify your true spiritual values, pointing you in the right direction. Even today, I still read books that I think can give me answers or show me new ideas.

Of course, there is (sadly!) no single miracle book with all the answers. But there are hundreds of books that can each give you an answer. Use those answers to make your own puzzle – both complex and unique to you. Even so, I'd like to offer a few suggestions for books that might help you effectively fill in your own 20%, as you find your way towards Egopreneurship.

WRITE YOUR OWN EULOGY

One of my all-time favourite books is *The Seven Habits of Highly Effective People* by the American author Stephen R. Covey. Not because it will make you highly effective (success in societal terms), but because it contains dozens of sentences that made me pause for thought and helped me keep my feet firmly on the ground. I've offered it as a present to a number of my athletes who were struggling to come to terms with the demands that their sport placed on them.

How many people are forced
to confess on their deathbed that
they didn't really live their life the way
they should have or wanted to?

One excellent suggestion from this book is that we should begin with the end in mind. You can only be effective if you know why you do what you do, if you're clear about where you want to go and you understand what's truly important to you. Covey shows us a great way to achieve this: 'Write your own eulogy and live up to its precepts.' What would you like your partner, friends, colleagues, family, etc. to say about you at your funeral? Thinking about your own funeral is perhaps not the most fun occupation, but it can help you to focus your mind on the best way to spend your remaining days. How many people confess on their deathbed that they didn't live their life the way they should have or intended to? How many are forced to admit that they had other (and better) plans that never came to fruition?

The message is clear: think about your personal mission. Draw up your own 'constitution' and let it shine through in the way you live. Not just today, but tomorrow and every day for the rest of your life. It is a constitution that's only reachable after numerous ups and downs, but even so, it's a marvellous tool to help you identify your most important 20%.

ASK WHY

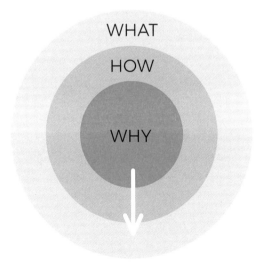

THE GOLDEN CIRCLE OF SIMON SINEK

My second book suggestion, *Start With Why,* by the Anglo-American organisational adviser Simon Sinek, follows the same basic idea. Using a series of simple concentric circles, Sinek succeeds in making it clear how to be successful in life, not in the sense of financial success, but in terms of leading a full and valued existence.

Sinek introduces the concept of the golden circle that describes a progression through life in three consecutive circles. It suggests that the most important of the three is the innermost circle: the why. It's only when you know your why that you can move outward to the next layer – the how – before reaching the outermost circle, the what. Unless you start from your why, with reason and purpose, you will never properly unveil how to achieve what you're looking for. This is the key to achieving that overarching life-goal that you hoped for.

I applied this principle in 1988, unconsciously, when I decided to begin coaching. It was never my intention to sell training programmes. I wanted to develop an approach to training that was different from the status quo. I wanted to coach athletes on the basis of the most recent scientific principles, a major departure from the rough and ready methods that were in vogue. That was my big 'why', the dream that motivated me.

To turn that dream into a reality, I converted my garage into a training centre and invested lots of money in all different kinds of (in my eyes) necessary equipment: a treadmill, an ergometer bike, devices to measure lactic acid and oxygen absorption, etc. I also spent a small fortune on developing my own training software. During this early period, my expenditure far exceeded my income, but I was the only trainer in Belgium with my own exercise laboratory. It was only after I discovered this 'how' that I moved on to compile training schedules to offer athletes from multiple disciplines at the highest levels.

STOP AND REFLECT!

It's not just management books like Sinek's that offer inspiration. Sometimes it's important to widen your perspective and search for insight in books that are more philosophical in nature. In a world where targets and work pressure are central, books of this kind can serve as a counterbalance.

This doesn't mean that you need to wrestle your way through heavy works like *The Critique of Pure Reason* by Immanuel Kant. It won't satisfy your search for your most important 20%. But exploring more accessible books, like *Philosophy for an Incomparable Life* by Lammert Kamphuis, can often be a source of unexpected motivation.

In his book, this Dutch philosopher makes the explicit link between philosophy and 'self-care': 'Philosophy can make your life more pleasant. By enriching your world with remarkable new perspectives, by making it easier to empathise with others, by challenging you to experiment with new ways of thinking and acting and by offering you thinking skills that will help you to take better care of yourself.'

In other words, from time to time it's necessary to stop and reflect, to see that your life isn't as much of a minefield as you may sometimes think. Another book that touches on this is *Reborn* by Majd Khalifeh. Khalifeh is best known in Belgium as the Middle Eastern and North African news specialist, working with the Flemish Broadcasting Company. At first glance he seems to epitomise an active Belgian citizen, a model for every newcomer to our country. But in his book, with its symbolic title, we accompany him on his search for meaning as a stateless Palestinian, who was forced to leave everything behind during his journey towards a new and fulfilling existence. Khalifeh expresses that sometimes we need to make 'tabula rasa' with our past to evoke a new essence of who and what we are.

MAYBE THINGS AREN'T SO BAD WITH THE WORLD AFTER ALL?

The next book gives perhaps an even bigger boost to your positive thinking: *Factfulness: Ten Reasons We're Wrong About the World and Why Things Are Better Than You Think*. Written by the Swedish doctor and professor of international health, Hans Rosling, it's a real eye-opener for everyone who thinks our world is going downhill at an ever-increasing pace. Rosling also seeks to give new direction to our thinking, which is often too linear. We all want to travel as quickly and as successfully as we can from point A to point B, but it's often more important to focus on the preconditions for achieving the solution to a problem, since that's often the most effective way to move further forward than we ever thought possible.

Rosling cites his experiences in Mozambique, where he once worked as a senior physician. He argues that to improve public health, don't start by investing in large hospitals. At first sight, this might sound controversial, certainly from a doctor. But when you read further, what he's saying becomes clear. It's better to use the available financial resources to train health workers, who can treat children in smaller local centres that are accessible to everyone. At the same time, invest in education, so that people can find better jobs and enjoy a higher standard of living making them less likely to need a hospital in the future.

Education and all other forms of training might seem like insignificant preconditions, but in the long run they can have a larger impact on people. That's also the kind of thinking that can help you to fill in your 20% in the best way possible.

DARE TO TAKE A STEP BACK

Gigantism, by Belgian economist Geert Noels, is another highly inspirational book for anyone who has the courage to focus on sustainability and more important things. Large companies and organisations are becoming ever more powerful, resulting in a non-stop upscaling that now sees the world bursting at its seams.

The economic impact of these developments is dramatic, commercial concentration, lack of competition and a complete change in societal behaviour. What's more, it's the individual who suffers most. For example: gigantism is responsible for huge increases in inequality and crime, as well as the growing incidence of so-called 'lifestyle diseases', like burn-out and obesity. People are finding that life is getting increasingly harder. How can they still hope to be effective? How can they identify and make best use of their strengths? How can they harness their best possible 20% so that they can maximise their results?

Geert Noels recommends that we stop constantly striving to acquire. Instead, we should take the time to stand still, to take a step back. It will allow us to identify the input for ourselves and for the people around us that offers the best return.

Whichever of these books you choose to read, they make it easier for you to fill in your 20% in the most effective way, while broadening your view of yourself and the world. They aren't 'heavy' literature, full of difficult language. They're accessible works that can really help. At the end of this chapter, you'll find an additional reading list of other potentially inspirational books.

You create sustainability
by regularly standing
still and daring to take
a step backwards.

Talking is silver, but silence is golden

It is not just books that can help you to harness your crucial 20% as a budding Egopreneur. Listening is also an important milestone for the development of your vision and values. This brings me back to Covey's *The Seven Habits of Highly Effective People*.

In his book, Covey argues that people will only understand you when you're able to understand them. Or as he puts it: 'Seek first to understand, then be understood.' Communication is much more than the transference of ideas and instructions. Understanding and targeting communication starts with empathic listening – to put yourself in the position of another.

However, empathic listening is both energy and time-consuming. And we're all lacking time, or rather, we're simply not allocating the time it takes to listen properly. It's important because people around us can be a huge source of inspiration, but we need to be open to receive it. Fortunately, none of us are an island, and your environment is not always the barrier that you might think it is.

Listening to other people's visions can help you to adjust or consolidate your own. The secret is to surround yourself with the right people, those who dare to be open and aren't superficial, but are prepared to share their vision with you.

Truly listening to others causes you to question your assumptions and helps you to free yourself from ideas that you've embedded into your thinking.

CHOOSE A GOOD SPARRING PARTNER

Listening is not a one-way process. Listening without reciprocation doesn't work. The people you surround yourself with must not only be worth listening to, but must be willing to listen to you in return. It's only when you exchange knowledge and ideas with others that the outcome can be valuable in your search for your 20%.

In effect, you become mental sparring partners, learning from each other and pushing each other to a higher level, following the aphorism that if you can't share what you have, you will never be able to multiply it. In this way, you become a touchstone for each other's values. Sometimes it's enough for my athletes to connect by phone. They know that they can call me whenever they want to let off steam, to put things in perspective, or just to listen to each other.

'WHAT DID YOU THINK OF MY TRAINING?'

The ability to both give and receive feedback is very important. Feedback makes us richer and gives us greater insight into how we can get the most out of our 20%.

In sport, giving feedback is something we do every day. For example, my cyclists register all their training sessions via a power meter. This meter automatically uploads details of each training ride or race onto a dedicated platform. This means that at the end of each day I have a clear picture of exactly what they have done: how much power they generated during each part of the ride or race, how fast they rode, how many meters of altitude they climbed, etc.

My cyclists are – rightly so – demanding and expect me to pay attention to details and provide them with prompt and useful feedback. When I speak to them on the phone, the first question they often ask is: 'What did you think of my training today?' As a result, I try to monitor their training efforts daily. Why? Because it's only when I give feedback that my athletes will learn. Only then will they be able to take the action necessary to make them even better. How can they improve otherwise?

'Feedback is food for champions' – an expression that every sports coach knows to be true. But giving feedback is by no means as evident as it sounds. Feedback can be a problem outside of sport, primarily because it's not always given in a constructive manner... This makes it even more difficult to accept that we need it.

FIND THE RIGHT SOUNDING BOARD

A sounding board that responds promptly, listens empathically and gives honest feedback is hugely important for everyone, especially for athletes. A coach is first and foremost a sounding board for the people they train. I've lost count of the times I've asked: 'how are you?', 'how was your training/race?', 'how did you sleep?', 'how is your knee, back, etc?'

After working with an athlete for some time, I occasionally become their mentor in addition to their trainer and coach. What's in a name? A world of difference. A trainer ensures that an athlete follows the right training programmes. A coach takes things to the next level by also devoting attention to the athlete's mental and physical development. But a mentor is yet something more, he's a mirror for the athlete. A mentor still gives technical guidance, but places that guidance and its significance in a much wider context. Essentially, he approaches the athlete as a human being in the broadest possible sense of the term. He'll be the one to always point to Sinek's 'golden why circle'. A mentor shouldn't be compared to a life alarm, but more precisely a warning light that flashes when you are in danger of straying from the right course.

There are certain phases in all our lives when we either need or must be a mentor. Paradoxically, when we take on the role of coach or mentor with the intention of helping others, we are still working on our own 'why' and are therefore putting Simon Sinek's golden circle into practice.

Don't set the bar too high

For your third touchstone, you need to ask yourself if you are setting yourself the right objectives. As a coach, I've almost always needed to put the brakes on my best athletes.

Athletes who are at the very top of their discipline put huge pressure on themselves. They want to perform to the very best of their ability, time after time. As a result, their coach needs to regularly rein them in to prevent them from going so far in training and/or competition that they exhaust their energy reserves. Of course, it's natural that athletes who are 200% motivated would continually ask more and more of themselves. It's precisely at this point that their coach needs to intervene, to ensure that their drive and passion are exercised with a necessary degree of restraint. We need to stop before our tanks run dry, before we hit a brick wall, before our ambition takes us too far and things start to go wrong.

It's not only in sport that you can see the effects of this issue. Regardless of the field of work, men and women at the top often have a tendency to set the bar ever higher. They too would benefit from being reined in, but sadly this doesn't always happen. We still see people who are convinced that better results can only be achieved by keeping up the pressure, even though they've already given the best of themselves and are stretched to the limits of their endurance.

Everybody has an ideal stress intensity zone, a zone in which he or she performs optimally. It's the task of a good coach to keep coachees just within the upper boundary of that zone. If pressure is applied above that boundary, its impact will be negative and level of performance will decline.

Don't get me wrong, extreme pressure and bars set too high will lead to harmful excess and ultimately failure. But that doesn't mean that there should be no pressure to perform. Consider 13- and 14-year-old adolescents. If they had no pressure to go to school, how many would show up on Monday morning, on Tuesday, on Wednesday…? Maybe by mid-week some would miss their friends and show up. By Thursday or Friday attendance levels would likely dip again as the weekend approached. Sounds like heaven? Perhaps it does to a teenager. Of course that also means that at year-end, few or perhaps none of the stay-at-homes would pass their exams.

Without stress, good performance is not possible.

THINK FOR THE SHORT TERM

Putting people under pressure to help them reach ambitious goals isn't without risk. The risk can also be managed by setting intermediary, short-term goals along the route to the primary objective. Aiming towards each of these successive goals at a time is much more realistic and will prevent you from feeling that you're always chasing rather than in control. This phased approach also means that your 20% will be better matched to your needs and abilities.

Remember – the journey is sometimes just as important as the destination. Think back to when Sven Nys was forced to give up during his mountain bike race at the summer Olympic Games in London in 2012. Afterwards, people asked him if he was disappointed because he didn't reach the finish line, let alone win a medal. They found it hard to believe that he was simply happy to have been part of the Olympic experience.

Naturally, Sven was initially disappointed when mechanical problems meant he had to pull out of the race. But the whole process leading up to the Games – including the difficulties he had in qualifying – was fascinating, enriching and ultimately a success. At one point it seemed that he would never make it to London at all. He finally qualified to participate less than three months before the opening of the Games. From this perspective, the journey itself – the battle to qualify – was an objective in its own right. Sven's participation in the medal race was, thus, an added bonus, a 'nice to have', but not a necessity.

It's also important to keep in mind that reaching your final objective is dependent on a multitude of factors outside your own effort and determination. A mountaineer may have years of experience and have prepared meticulously, but if the weather turns against him on the day of the climb he will never get to the top. There are some things in life you simply have to accept. Acceptance is much easier if you avoid linking your sense of identity too closely to the achievement of a single objective.

Once bitten, twice shy

The path to success should be designed with care, meaning that intermediary objectives shouldn't be plucked out of thin air. Remember your mistakes and learn from them. Over the years, you've built up a store of knowledge and experience, so use it wisely. Far too many people seem to eradicate all memories from their past. Not just the negative things, but many times the positive. This is a recipe for making the same mistake over and over again.

During my coaching career, I have been confronted on numerous occasions with various new gadgets and trends that have been said to influence performance such as diet, equipment and training methods. Each time, I was promised 'significant improvements' in athlete performance. Actual result? Zero! Hypoxic training, low-carb training, empty stomach training, pure chocolate and beetroot diets, dietary supplements, five pieces of fruit a day, three pieces of fruit a day, etc. I have seen these fads come and go. In time I learned not to ignore them, per se, but to take them with a large pinch of salt. I evaluated their usefulness, but continued concentrating on the basics that I valued through experience: training hard but responsibly, giving due attention to my athletes as human beings with physical and mental limitations, even accepting limits in their outstanding abilities. I never forgot these basic lessons and I think I can say that it has served my athletes and me very well.

All too often, we have a tendency to put our heads down and keep on ploughing forward, following the same old routine day after day, just like a hamster on a treadmill. What we should be doing is pausing occasionally for thought and self-reflection. We need to step off the treadmill and exchange its narrow view for a more expansive bird's-eye view, allowing us to see our life and our objectives more clearly.

By questioning things and by using your
experience to adjust your objectives accordingly,
you can give yourself a real bonus.

Perhaps this problem is typical for the age in which we live. People make too little time for themselves. They are continually in action mode, searching for the next objective, striving for the ultimate performance. As a result, they are constantly getting ahead of themselves until they eventually run into a brick wall. You'll often hear them say: 'But I don't have the time for standing still or for reflection. Do you have any idea how many things I need to do? What they need to realise is that with this so-called lost time there comes huge long-term benefit. By questioning things and using experience to adjust objectives accordingly, you can give yourself a real bonus. So, do yourself a favour and step off the treadmill, slow down and decide where you really want to go in life.

Accept reality

In the 21st century, where everything is supposed to be possible, our final touchstone is perhaps the most difficult of all: acceptance. It's not always possible to achieve 100% of what you want. You can't be the best at everything. It's simply not feasible. What's more, it's not necessary. Striving for perfection will only make you unhappy. You'll put so much pressure on yourself that even the pleasant things in life will become an intolerable burden. When this happens, burn-out is never far away.

You don't always have to try and reach the top. It's not necessary to claw your way to the highest rung on the hierarchical ladder, to get the top job. What's important is to achieve your personal 'top performance' in the position you are currently occupying. You need to feel yourself growing and developing within the boundaries of this position, so that you eventually become a leader for the other people you work with. Not a leader in the traditional, hierarchical sense of the word, but a leader as someone who shares his knowledge with others and gives them the opportunity to grow and develop alongside you, while learning to accept that there are some things you'll never be able to change.

My suggestion is to adopt an attitude of stoicism. By this I don't mean that you should become complacent or fatalistic. Quite the contrary. A stoic outlook involves doing your best, while realising that not everything is within your reach. Or as the Stoic philosopher Epicurus wrote, 'do not spoil what you have by desiring what you have not. Remember that what you now have was once among the things you only hoped for.' In other words, embrace acceptance as a fundamental principle in your life, while remembering that you are still capable of accomplishing a great deal.

All the above touchstones will help you fill in your 20% in the best, most appropriate way for you. They have certainly all been relevant for me. But bear in mind that it's not a one-off exercise. You need to keep revising and amending your 20% as you evolve throughout your life.

Why did I regularly hesitate to accept offers to coach various top athletes? It was certainly not because I didn't believe in them. It was first and foremost because I wanted to reflect on whether I could provide them with the 20% of myself that was necessary. I wanted to avoid making a hasty decision that we might later regret by analysing the situation thoroughly in advance. I wanted to see whether their expectations for our collaboration were compatible with the way I saw my own life. I believed that 'no' should be the initial starting point from which – after further ripe reflection – it might be possible to move towards a much more realistic 'yes'.

My personal reading list

- » Enlightenment Now. *Steven Pinker*
- » Brain Chains. *Theo Compernolle*
- » Busy. *Tony Crabbe*
- » The Gold Mine Effect. *Rasmus Ankersen*
- » Legacy. *James Kerr*
- » Stress Proof. *Mithu Storoni*
- » Outliers. *Malcolm Gladwell*
- » We are Our Brains. *Dick Swaab*
- » Homo Deus. *Yuval Noah Harari*
- » Why the World Isn't Going to the Dogs. *Maarten Boudry*

- » Thinking, Fast and Slow. *Daniel Kahneman*

Your supplementary list:

- » ....
- » ....
- » ....
- » ....
- » ....
- . . .

4

The right combination

Energy Lab launched a talent search in 2010. We identified young cycling talent and offered them a programme of intensive guidance and training that would prepare them for a possible professional career in cycling. One of the young and ambitious riders who came under my charge at this time was Tim Wellens. He was chomping at the bit and couldn't wait to take the cycling world by storm. He wanted to move forward, and fast! But I had different ideas.

To make things absolutely clear, let me repeat what I've already said: as an Ego-preneur, the ideal 20% to spend on a project or on yourself doesn't exist. Not for you, not for me, not for anyone. The world is complex and we are always on the move. We need to take account of the continually changing processes around us.

For some people, this can have a debilitating effect. Why do we have to be constantly changing and adjusting? Once we've made our plan, why can't it remain intact, engraved as it were, in tablets of stone? Because, in practice, we find that perpetual variability is highly advantageous. Retaining the option to change means that no single decision is ever final, that we can revise that decision, in light of the broader picture.

What seems ideal today may not be appropriate or effective tomorrow. We need to be able to deal with the concept of transformation and accept that we are living in volatile times. Exactly how do we do this?

Positive change

I found important advice on how to exercise a process of non-stop change in a positive way in the work of Rosabeth Moss Kanter. Kanter is an American professor of sociology (at the Harvard Business School), who believes that organisations can only work efficiently if they have a holistic vision and are open to positive change. In her TEDx Talk (which can be found on YouTube under 'Rosabeth Moss Kanter at TEDx Beacon Street'), she refers to the six keys leading to positive change. These six keys are as follows:

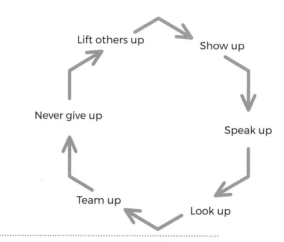

THE SIX KEYS FOR POSITIVE CHANGE ACCORDING TO ROSABETH MOSS KANTER

➜ SHOW UP

Don't hide in the shadows. Stand up and be counted. If you fail to do that, things will never change. You must make yourself available and must realise that your presence can make the difference.

➜ SPEAK UP

It is crucial to use the power of your voice. People cannot know what you are thinking unless you make it clear to them. But the power of your voice isn't just about the words that you speak. It's also about addressing and redefining the agendas and problems of others, so that you help them to think differently about those agendas and problems.

> Proactive people can
> make the difference.
> A reactive approach
> gets you nowhere.

The people with greatest impact are those who have the courage and the ability to clearly identify and name the problem and who then encourage others to take the necessary action. You help no-one if you see a problem and think things will go wrong, but say nothing until it's too late.

'Show up' and 'speak up' are vitally important. If things do go wrong, you will often hear people say: 'I saw this coming'. It's a reactive approach that benefits nobody. Proactivity can be and make the difference.

→ LOOK UP

If you want to change things in a positive way, do so on the basis of a higher value or vision. You have to know and should let others know precisely what you stand for. Based on your values and vision, you must then be able to inspire people to move to a higher level.

It's vital in both the world of business and sport that certain values are respected. But it's not always easy. If a rider like Tim Wellens says loud and clear that doping-free cycling is his first and most important priority, condemning the use of doping in all its forms, including the grey area of admissible medication, then it is worth noting that regrettably not everyone in the cycling entourage responds with enthusiasm, even though it's only by adopting this kind of values-based approach that the sport will finally be able to put doping behind it.

→ TEAM UP

Everything works better if you surround yourself with the right people. It's difficult to achieve anything that is worth it, on your own. The best projects begin with partnership.

I have always been aware that as a coach I am part of a whole, a gear in a much bigger machine. With any sporting victory, the lion's share of the credit must go to the athlete. But he/she would be unable to succeed without the contributions of many other people. It's the same with coaching outside of sport. The idea that a coach can do everything for a coachee is unrealistic. It simply doesn't work.

➜ NEVER GIVE UP

There will be times in your project when everything you want to do, all the positive changes you wish to introduce, look like they will fail. It's very rare to bring something worthwhile to a successful conclusion without the need to overcome obstacles somewhere along the way. So never give up. No matter the difficulties – keep pressing on. Perseverance is a key characteristic of successful people.

Whenever I start a new coaching trajectory with an athlete, I always say that I will need a full two years before our collaboration becomes optimal. It takes time to get to know my athletes to understand how they react in certain situations. I know in advance that we will meet difficulties and that things won't always go as planned. Of course I'm always prepared to adapt my approach to circumstance, to these difficulties, but in return I expect my coachee to maintain trust in me and to stick to the programme we agreed upon.

➜ LIFT OTHERS UP

If you want to change things, it's crucial to share your success. Recognise the contributions made by those who've helped you and give them credit where credit is due. This supports an environment in which success can be repeated.

As you can see, everything is connected to everything else, and it is important that this reciprocal process is kept in motion. 'Standing still is going backwards' – it's an old cliché, but one that is more valid than ever in these changing times.

Success without overcoming
obstacles is a utopia.

Filling in your 20%

When seeking to fill in your precious 20%, there are a number of factors that should be taken into account. Focus on activities that are realistic, manageable and challenging – those that will broaden your perspective.

DO NOT OVERDO IT

When deciding what to do with your 20%, it's important to set realistic objectives and accept your limits. Later in this book we'll look in detail at the importance of exercise, a critical part of your development as an Egopreneur.

A few years ago, a doctor in a local town and its residents resolved to create a healthier community. They initiated a 'Start to Run' project and immediately saw impressive results. But what happened then? A number of the participants, encouraged by their early progress, went beyond the limits set in the agreed training programme. As a result, they overtaxed their bodies and ended up with strain injuries. Within a few weeks, the doctor saw no fewer than 82 such patients! Most of them blamed their injuries on the programme and dropped out. But the problem was not the programme. The problem was that the inexperienced runners had failed to follow the programme correctly. The moral of the story is that if you want to improve your health and fitness, working realistically is a top priority.

TAKE SMALL STEPS

'Successful people dare to think big.' How often have we heard that when praising the successes of the world's great achievers? But is this actually a valid general rule and the best approach? We all know the great success stories of people like Steve Jobs and Elon Musk. But do we ever hear about the countless others who 'dared to think big' and fell flat on their face?

I have no faith in this 'the sky is the limit' philosophy. There are smarter and safer ways to achieve your objectives. What's the point of deciding that your goal is to climb Mount Everest, if you know in your heart of hearts that you will never be able to achieve it? Instead, why not divide up your objective into a series of smaller, more manageable climbs? Start with a trek through the foothills and build up to greater heights. In the beginning, don't be afraid to set your sights lower.

If your objectives are too big, you will quickly lose control of the process and become overwhelmed by your ambition before you've even started. For example, too many people who want to work at reducing their weight set objectives like: 'I want to lose 10 to 15 kilograms, preferably within x weeks.' Every evening they tell themselves that they are going to start their diet tomorrow and hope to shed at least three kilograms during the first week. But by the end of the next day they have overeaten or not exercised and vow to 'really' start tomorrow. They aren't prepared to take the necessary trek through the foothills, they go directly to the summit of Everest. But what they need to do is set a target of losing one or two kilograms each month, a much more manageable and sustainable target. If they persevere, they will eventually see the summit, keep getting closer, and eventually achieve their goal.

Thinking big is no guarantee of success.

MORE THAN YOUR LAST BREATH

Of course, this doesn't mean that you shouldn't set objectives that are challenging, that test your limits. 'If everything seems under control, you're just not going fast enough.' These are the legendary worlds spoken by racing driver Mario Andretti, 1978 Formula 1 world champion, when someone asked him to explain the secret of his success. After his impressive victory in the 2019 Amstel Gold Race, Dutch cyclist Mathieu van der Poel posted something similar on social media: 'You've gotta want it more than your last breath.'

In other words, it's not necessary to have everything always fully under control. You have to strike the right balance between challenge and realism. It's only when you leave your comfort zone that you will be able to push yourself to a higher level. In other words, set objectives that are testing, but still realistically feasible. This is the only way to initiate change.

PERSPECTIVES

As an Egopreneur in the making, when you define the content of your 20%, make sure that it includes objectives and/or activities that will be relevant for the future. If your objectives aren't relevant once you achieve them, then your 20% has little real substance and no long-term viability.

People don't continue to work with satisfaction if they can see no relevance in what they do. We aren't machines that continue working regardless. We are sentient beings, who ask ourselves questions. Why am I doing this? What will it achieve? Where will it lead me?

Obstacles

Sometimes you will fail to successfully complete your important 20%. Instead of implementing it as hoped, you won't get beyond the planning phases. How come? What's keeping you from reaching your objectives?

THE DESIRE FOR STABILITY

Human beings are organisms, which means that we are subject to what biologists call homeostasis. Our autonomic homeostasis mechanism ensures that vital bodily functions such as blood pressure, breathing, temperature, etc., remain in a state of equilibrium. If this equilibrium is disturbed, the body will do everything possible to restore it.

If the body remains out of balance, our health can be at risk. This is first and foremost a physiological process, but it has a psychological equivalent – a kind of mental homeostasis. This means that we have a natural tendency to prefer the stability of what we know. We like things to be familiar and 'ordinary'. And when it comes to change, people are instinctively uncomfortable with it.

> If you ever want to achieve anything,
> you have to come out of your comfort zone.

In this way, our brain is programmed to behave conservatively – like an overprotective parent immediately eliminating anything that might put our safety or stability at risk, including things that can lead to positive change.

Because the nature of our optimal 20% is constantly changing, this process of psychological homeostasis complicates our search for the most ideal activities to engage our 20%. As a result, we often find ourselves torn by indecision, so that we end up rejecting change.

As a coach for top athletes, I am well aware of the importance of interrupting homeostasis, both physical and mental. I repeat: if you ever want to achieve anything, you have to come out of your comfort zone. If you always train with the same consistent degree of intensity, you fail to give your body the stimulation it needs to move to the next level. As a result, your performance will stagnate and eventually fall back, instead of continuing to improve.

Change is a necessary component of your 20%, meaning you must try new things and let go of what may have worked for you in the past. But don't over-do it, otherwise you risk knocking your natural homeostasis completely out of balance, which is never a good thing. It's a bit like walking a tightrope of new possibilities: just don't fall off!

A (TEMPORARY) LACK OF ENTHUSIASM

You work hard all week. You never seem to have a moment for yourself. Every second counts. You can feel the hot breath of your overfull agenda on your neck. And then, thank God it's Sunday! A free day in your diary! But to do what?

Does this mean catching up on your sleep? Or perhaps some sport? Maybe even a little puttering around the house? Or do you find it impossible to empty your mind, so that you plan all kinds of things but end up doing none of them, apart from eating badly, drinking too much, and sleeping restlessly – again?

In other words, you do nothing, but not because you chose to do nothing: it 'just happened', because of your lethargy and indifference. There is nothing positive about this kind of indecisiveness. In fact, it is often a prelude to a downwards spiral that will see your attitude becoming increasingly negative.

One possible solution is to adopt Mel Robbins' five second rule. This author of the bestseller suggests that whenever a good idea for a new objective pops into your head, you should take a positive action to put it into effect within five seconds. If you fail to do so, your brain will automatically 'kill' the idea.

For example, imagine an idea coming to mind, not a foolish one that you will never be able to implement, but something connected to a feasible objective, whether great or small. It's a bit like a door opening inside your brain. According to Robbins, you need to see that door, walk through it and take control of the situation, and all before you have counted 'one, two, three, four, and five.' Now that's taking the bull by the horns!

Of course, you also need to remember that consciously doing nothing, even boring yourself for an hour or two, can have an inspirational effect. In his book *De Wachter's World*, the well-known Belgian psychiatrist Dirk De Wachter described the importance of having a little boredom in your life. Just sitting and thinking, about everything and nothing. Or wandering aimlessly along the beach or through the woods. He proposed that this kind of boredom is fulfilling.

LACK OF DISCIPLINE

'He has talent, but lacks discipline.' This comment I hear far too often as a coach. Discipline is not only important in sport. In his manual entitled *Scenario schrijven* (*Writing a Screenplay*), the Belgian playwright Marc Didden proposed that writers need to develop a stubborn streak: 'Because writing is 1% inspiration and 99% discipline.'

It also takes discipline to make concrete plans for your 20% and effectively implement them. The obstacles we have already mentioned may conspire to ensure that your 20% gets you precisely nowhere, so that you remain locked in the homeostatic grip of your easy and familiar way of life.

As a coach, I have trained plenty of people who know precisely what discipline is. They stick to their plan, no matter what. Even if it is pouring down outside, they do their daily miles. Even if they are having a fun time with their teammates in a hotel, they get to bed on time. They also know that a time-out is important every now and then. But above all, they know that the frequency and intensity of their training must be maintained if they want to be successful. And that requires just one thing: discipline.

THE EISENHOWER MATRIX

You will have noticed by now that it is not always easy to do the right thing at the right time. Equally, it is not always easy to prevent homeostasis from per-suading you to fall back into old and familiar habits. Yet, the ability to overcome these hindrances so that you can do the right thing at the right time is crucial to make the best use of your 20%.

A practical tool to support decision-making is the Eisenhower matrix, named after former American president Dwight D. Eisenhower. It's based on his com-ment: *'I have two kinds of problems, the urgent and the important. The urgent are not important, and the important are never urgent.'*

This results in a matrix with four different quadrants: urgent and important; non-urgent and important; urgent and unimportant; and non-urgent and un-important.

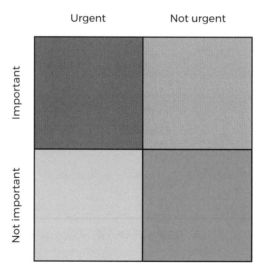

THE EISENHOWER MATRIX

On which of the four quadrants should you focus? People often answer, urgent and important. For example, after a visit to the doctor it becomes apparent that there is something not quite right with your blood values. Your pressure is high and you have too much cholesterol and blood sugar. The advice the doctor gives you is important and needs to be followed urgently: a change of diet and more daily exercise. In other words, you have no choice (if you want to live).

But is that the quadrant you need to focus on every day? No, of course not. Your main focus should be on things that are non urgent but important. For example, everyone knows that exercise is important, but is it really urgent? No, not really. You can start next week, next month or as part of your New Year's resolution. But if you keep on postponing it, you may find yourself in front of the doctor, when his advice changes the situation to important <u>and</u> urgent.

Here's another example. Students know that studying is important. But in November it's not urgent, as exams are still a long way off. But it's different in May, when the exams are just weeks away. Studying suddenly becomes super-important and super-urgent. But what if the student had already begun to study regularly from November onwards? Would it still be super-urgent in May?

The message should be clear: place your focus on non-urgent but important matters. In this way, the number of matters that are urgent will quickly become much reduced.

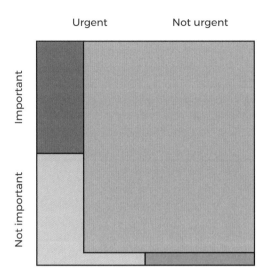

Urgent   Not urgent

Important

Not important

THE EISENHOWER MATRIX, WITH THE FOCUS ON 'IMPORTANT BUT NON-URGENT MATTERS'

Useful? Certainly. Even so, you need to remember that choosing your right 20% is not something that will happen all by itself. You need to work at it – and work at it hard.

I have been working with Tim Wellens for 10 years. During that time, he has evolved into a top-class cyclist, a real winner. From the very first day of our collaboration my motto was step by step. We set no major objectives, other than to improve year by year, so that we could create a solid platform for further progress. So far, this has worked very well for us, although there have been periods when things went less well than we had expected.

But it's precisely at those moments that you need to hold on to your vision. Get back up, dust yourself off and start all over again. Tim's progress is also rooted in a value that is very important for us both: a strict respect for the rules of the sport. In this context, there is only black and white. No grey.

Questions

» Do you dare to step forward and speak
  when it is necessary?

» How realistic is the content of your 20% as
  an Egopreneur?

» Do you sometimes leave your comfort
  zone?

» Do you make a distinction between things
  that are important and urgent and things
  that are important but not urgent?

PART 2

5

Body and mind

Go down to your local running track. Try and run a 400 metre lap in one minute and nine seconds. There is a strong chance that you won't be able to do it. You can? Good for you! Now try and run a kilometre (two and a half laps) at the same pace. If you succeed, this means that you covered the kilometre in two minutes and fifty-three seconds. You are still keeping up? That would surprise me, because to run a kilometre at a speed of 20 kilometres and 81 metres per hour means that you must be a very good runner. If you can keep that up for five kilometres, you would cover the distance in 14 minutes and 25 seconds. Are you feeling dizzy yet?

Well, that is exactly the pace that the Kenyan super-athlete Eliud Kipchoge was able to keep up in Berlin over the full distance of the marathon: 42 kilometres and 195 metres. A phenomenal, mind-boggling performance. He crossed the finishing line with a broad smile on his face, only then to fall into the arms of his coach and mentor, Patrick Sang, a former Olympic medallist himself in the steeplechase.

When I studied physical education at KU Leuven, one of my professors was Edmond 'Mon' Vanden Eynde. Mon was an almost legendary athletics trainer, with multiple Olympic medal winners and world record holders among his athletes. At Leuven, he taught training principles and sports psychology.

At the time, there were wild stories about his training methods. For example, it was said that during the short periods of recuperation in interval training he would force his athletes to stand up to their midriffs in the ice-cold waters of the River Dijle, which ran alongside the track. Why? Because he wanted to hinder the discharge of waste products from his athletes' muscles.

Apart from these stories, which may or may not have been true, we never knew, we learned very little about the real ins and outs of Mon's personal training methods. He was, unfortunately, reluctant to talk about them.

However, there was one comment Mon made that I have never forgotten and it has become the fundamental principle on which I base all my coaching, both inside and outside of sport: 'A coach that can master the principles of super-compensation will be the best coach in the world. But be warned, there is no principle more difficult to master.'

To understand this, we must first start in the world of competitive sport, before applying it to our daily lives.

The universal principle of super-compensation

The principle of super-compensation says that your performance level deteriorates as a result of training. Does that sound a bit odd? Perhaps. But imagine if training would always make you fitter, faster, stronger, etc. If that were true, then all you would ever need to do is train, train and train again. More and more, harder and harder, so that you became better and better. But that's not how it works.

Anyone with knowledge on the principles of training, any experienced athlete, knows that the quickest way to lose your fitness is to train too much, too hard. After a hard training session, you are tired. Your muscles will have suffered and you sometimes feel on the verge of exhaustion.

At that moment, your level of performance has not increased, but decreased. Previous training sessions will have had a positive effect on performance, but only if training was followed by sufficient periods of recovery. What's more, if you allow your body to recover sufficiently after training, your fitness will not only return to its previous level from before the training, but will actually have improved a little, taking your overall fitness slightly higher. This marginal gain from training is known as super-compensation. You can therefore reach your best level of fitness and performance by constantly repeating this cycle: training-recovery-super-compensation. The following image makes this clear.

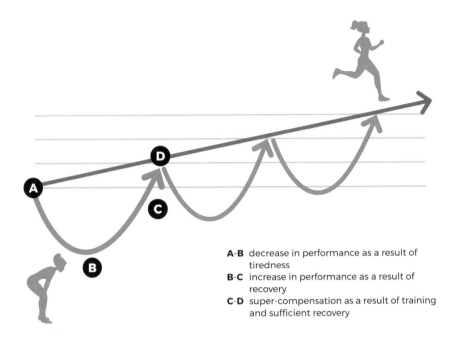

A-B decrease in performance as a result of tiredness
B-C increase in performance as a result of recovery
C-D super-compensation as a result of training and sufficient recovery

THE PRINCIPLE OF SUPER-COMPENSATION

The benefits of super-compensation can be measured in an enhanced function of the cardiac and respiratory systems, and in your muscles. In other words, you can make a muscle stronger by first tiring it out, and then nourishing it and allowing it to recover. This makes the muscle bigger and stronger, so that its overall endurance increases.

The length of time an athlete needs to recover after training is dependent on many different factors, such as the current level of fitness and the length and intensity of the training. An athlete who is already in good condition recovers more quickly. Factors like food, sleep and mental status also play a significant role. The importance of an individual's mental status is often neglected. I believe strongly in the indisputable link between our mental and physical selves. I have seen on countless occasions, mentally strong athletes recover quicker after hard training. On the other hand, this means that anxious athletes will recovery more slowly.

The following diagram shows what happens if you fail to recover sufficiently:

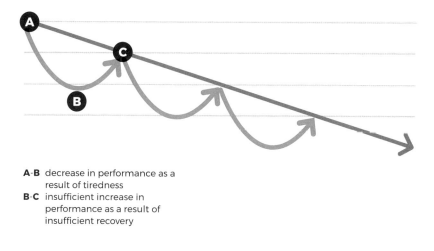

A-B decrease in performance as a
result of tiredness
B-C insufficient increase in
performance as a result of
insufficient recovery

THE PRINCIPLE OF SUPER-COMPENSATION IN THE EVENT OF INSUFFICIENT RECOVERY

In the above case, training was restarted too soon – before there was sufficient recovery, allowing super-compensation to have its positive effect. As a result, the athlete's physical condition went rapidly downhill instead of improving. If this situation were to continue for too long, a state of chronic overtraining would be reached and a long period of recovery would be needed to regain lost fitness.

The principle of super-compensation is generally accepted in the sporting world. However, applying it correctly is extremely difficult because of the sheer number of factors that can influence it: the nature of the training, the athlete's level of fitness, the recovery time, diet, sleep, mental condition, etc. Mental condition can also be influenced by a host of additional factors over which a coach has little or no control, even if they are aware of them (which is not always the case). This might include, for example, relationship problems, the athlete's social environment, etc. For these reasons, it's vital for me as a coach to have as much contact with my athletes as I can and to listen carefully to what they have to say. If, for example, I sense that an athlete is not sleeping well, has lost their appetite, is not giving 100% in training or is more irritable than usual, an alarm bell immediately sounds in my head.

This means that to keep an athlete performing at the top level is more often a question of focusing on factors that have nothing to do with training than on the actual training schedule itself. The take-home message is that to keep an athlete at peak performance, a coach needs to manage numerous factors that have little to do with the training itself.

JUST LIKE AN ATHLETE

Let's now make the leap from elite athletes to our daily lives. If you look at the following image you will see that it is quite similar to the last one.

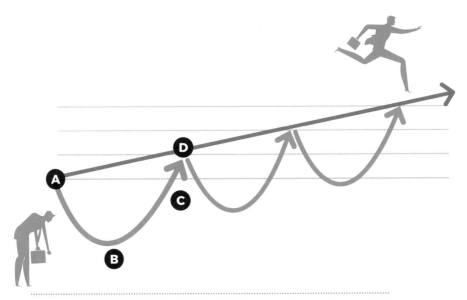

THE PRINCIPLE OF SUPER-COMPENSATION APPLIED TO DAILY LIFE

In fact, during your daily life with all its (work-related) trials and tribulations, you are just like an athlete. In the evening, at the end of your work day, you feel worse than when you started in the morning. Your daily workload and the associated stress tires you and robs you of energy. You may even feel that you are nearing exhaustion.

If it's a comfort, there is nothing wrong with feeling that way. It is impossible to ride the crest of the wave. Even the very best surfers have wipe-outs and need to find a new wave. Sometimes you can find it quickly sometimes you need to wait. But eventually it comes along.

So it's not a problem if your work pulls you out of your comfort zone. In fact, it is essential! If everything is always easy and goes to plan, you will never make any progress. You will never get better, because you will never have had to solve any problems.

Like athletes, Egopreneurs need time to recover, so that they can progress to a higher level. Your brain reacts in the same way as an athlete's muscle. It becomes stronger if it's first drained and then given time to recharge its batteries.

TIPPING POINT

In other words, there is nothing wrong with experiencing some stress during the day and feeling tired in the evening. You need stress in order to be able to perform. But as the following diagram makes clear, you don't want to overdo it.

The Stress Model

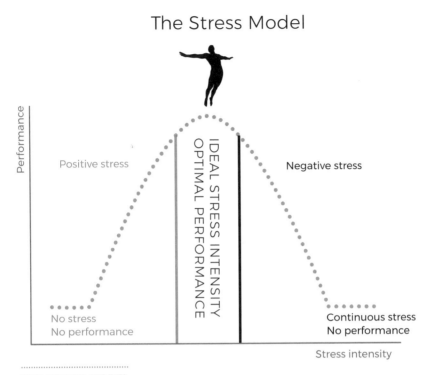

THE STRESS MODEL

As you can see, increases in performance and stress levels are positively correlated, but only up to a certain point. This so-called tipping point marks the moment when positive stress becomes negative stress, so that performance starts to fall off. If the level of stress continues to rise past the tipping point, performance becomes difficult or even impossible and burn-out is likely.

No-one is capable of dealing with continuous stress. An example from the world of sport: at the end of 2005 the Russian world champion and world-record holder in pole vaulting, Yelena Isinbayeva, found herself unexpectedly confronted with the physical and mental limits of her extraordinary capabilities. In the previous seasons she had won more or less everything there was to win. She suddenly became overwhelmed by the pressure of always having to be the best, of always having to raise the bar (literally in her case). She was in urgent need of rest and change in her approach to training if she was to get back to her best form.

As illustrated by the stress model:

» Never go beyond your tipping point for long and continuous periods. Make sure you regularly include periods of recovery in your agenda. If you find yourself on the right-hand side of the curve for too long, you will descend into a downward spiral. Continual stress over a long period inevitably leads to the (total) breakdown of your ability to perform.

» Everyone has his/her individual tipping point. Some people are more stress-resistant than others. However, it is possible to move your tipping point further to the right by working to improve your mental resilience. In a later chapter we'll examine how Egopreneurs can improve their mental resilience.

My experience with top athletes has taught me that the best in the business are always positioned to the right of the curve. In other words, they always put lots of (and sometimes too much) pressure on themselves. As mentioned previously, a large part of my job as a coach is to make sure that this pressure is maintained at an acceptable level.

The tipping point phenomena is not exclusive to the sporting world, nor is it limited to people of any particular mind-set or walk of life. Men and women at the top always need to be told to slow down, simply to prevent them from overdoing it. This is very different from the misguided belief, held by some, that results can only be achieved under conditions of continued stress. In reality, this approach is little more than a recipe for losing good people.

Fight or flight

Today, many people experience stress as a harmful influence in their lives. As a result, stress has assumed negative connotations. But as we've already seen, this is not entirely justified. Stress can sometimes be beneficial. In fact, without our stress hormones – the most important of which are cortisol, noradrenaline and adrenaline – life wouldn't be possible.

When we're faced with a demanding, unexpected, unusual, tense, dangerous or negative situation, our body releases stress hormones. In other words, these hormones are first and foremost part of the body's defence mechanism. They bring the body to a heightened state of awareness, preparing us to deal with the threat that confronts us.

More sugar is released into our blood, so that we temporarily have more energy to remain alert and respond effectively to the stressful situation. At the same time, our heart rate and blood pressure increase, and our muscles tense. Put simply, stress hormones make us ready to fight or flee.

This physiological process has likely already saved your life. Think, for example, of the speed of your reactions when you are riding your bike and you suddenly see a car hurtling towards you. Almost before you realise it, the effect of your stress hormones allows you to react instantly by hitting the brakes, turning your handlebars and digging your heels into the ground.

The effect of stress hormones can persist for quite some time. This explains why it can be hard to get to sleep at night after a particularly stressful day. And it makes no difference whether that stress was positive or negative. It can happen to an athlete who has won or lost. Or to a teacher who continues to wonder, after hours of school meetings, whether the advice they gave was actually best for their pupils. In all these cases, the correct hormone balance has not yet been restored by the time the athlete or teacher is ready to go to sleep. As a result, the feeling of nervous tension has not yet dissipated.

ME? STRESS? NEVER!

When I ask a group of business people if they have ever had problems with stress, very few of them voluntarily admit it. It is only when the first couple of hands tentatively appear that a few more might follow, but that's often all. People continue to find it tough or macho to profile themselves as super-stress-resistant, as someone who always has everything (including himself or herself) under control, at all times.

I'm afraid I just don't believe them. If we consider the number and the nature of the factors that can cause negative stress, it's impossible that people are immune to them. Scientific research has shown that we only have very limited, if any, control over the physiological process that activates our stress hormone.

I do believe that some people are more stress-resistant than others, that some others also experience stress in a more positive way. But to state that some people never have stress: that's taking things too far. Everyone is subject to the impact of stress, to a greater or lesser degree.

The denial or suppression of stress has a lot to do with the pattern of expectations in our modern-day society. People think it is good to be stress-resistant, whereas succumbing to stress is often frowned upon. As a result, the social pressure to be stress-resistant is considerable. If someone is unwilling to admit that they have a problem with stress, it is difficult to take the necessary corrective action to restore the balance between their stress load and capacity.

The balance between stress load and capacity

Stressors continually disrupt the balance between the stress load you experience and your capacity to deal with that stress. If this balance is negative only occasionally and/or for relatively short periods, it shouldn't be a problem. On the contrary, the temporary disruption of your balance can keep you on your toes and push you to a higher level of performance.

If, however, your stress balance is permanently disrupted, things will soon start to go wrong and you will find yourself with a serious problem. Continual exposure to stress factors means that the neuro-physiological system that produces your stress hormones is never allowed to rest. It is more or less in constant operation, as a result of which your pattern of sleep is seriously disturbed. And if you are unable to sleep, recovery becomes very difficult, forcing you to draw too heavily on your body's finite resources. Ultimately, this can lead to both physical complaints and mental exhaustion.

As a budding Egopreneur, it's important that you are able to recognise the symptoms of negative stress at an early stage. But that, by itself, is not enough. You must first be willing to admit to yourself and to others that something isn't right.

HOLIDAY AT LAST! AND THEN...

Have you ever noticed how many people get sick as soon as their holiday starts? A possible reason is that the level of stress at work often reaches a peak immediately before a holiday. There are seemingly endless things to finish before we disappear for a fortnight! As a result, you work like a lunatic right up to the very last moment, so that you can leave with a clear conscience. This means that by the time you actually set off for France or Spain or wherever it might be, you are nearing the point of exhaustion. Consequently, your resistance to infection is weakened, so that mild everyday viruses are enough to make you ill. Another possible explanation is that people tend to fight against their tiredness and reduced resistance until the day their vacation arrives. Once they no longer need to cope with pressure they decompress, they tire, their resistance drops and they fall ill.

I (DON'T) FEEL FINE

I have always kept a close lookout for signals from my coachees that might indicate a disrupted balance between their (training) load and capacity. If one of my athletes arrives for training with a cold sore (herpes) on his lip, I know immediately that this means I need to cut down the training for a day or two or even cancel it altogether, even if the athlete in question tells me that they feel fine, which is usually the case. I never let them convince me to carry on training at the same level. Top athletes always want to train and to train hard, because they know that the dividing line between performance improvement and performance deterioration is a fine one.

Herpes only manifests itself when the training load has been exceeded by too much and/or for too long. When this happens, the immune system is less resistant to the herpes virus. Reduced immunity is nearly always the result of long-term physical and/or mental stress. In these circumstances, the first and only thing a coach can do is to oblige the athlete to rest.

In addition to reduced immunity, there are a number of other physical signals that can indicate the onset of negative stress: head and neck pain, pain in the shoulders, hyperventilation, digestive disorders, disrupted patterns of sleep, anxiety, chest pain, heart complaints, stomach and intestinal complaints, libidinal issues. Sometimes it is even possible for new medical conditions to emerge in response to stress overload, such as allergies or asthma.

If the negative stress is long term, the symptoms can exhibit themselves in an even wider variety of ways: loss of concentration, reduced creativity, forgetfulness, increased irritability, sleeping problems, communication difficulties, relational complications, increased absence from work, etc. The effects of chronic exposure to stress are varied and can be profound.

Taking your stress-resistance to a higher level

The number of possible stress factors is almost endless: targets and deadlines that need to be met, conflicts with colleagues and superiors, bullying, job uncertainty, overwork, lack of feedback, too much work, not enough work, perfectionism, noise pollution, illness in your personal environment, social media overload, exaggerated expectation, promotion, demotion, a negative self-image, an imbalance between your work and your private life, unexpected telephone calls or visitors, poor results, unresolved traumas, getting older – just to name a few!

It is not possible to eliminate stress factors.
Concentrate instead on improving
your stress resistance.

It should by now be clear that stress can have its origins in every part of your life. Even matters that at first glance seem positive can easily become the source of negative stress. For example, success often brings with it a whole range of new obligations and commitments and the stress to perpetuate that success can sometimes have a debilitating effect.

It should be equally clear that it is very difficult or even impossible to control all the possible stressors, so that stress can hit anyone unexpectedly at any time of the day. Also, once one stressor disappears, another one often arrives almost instantly to take its place.

Rather than trying to eliminate stressors, which is simply not possible, we should focus instead on trying to increase our stress resistance. People have different resistance levels and not everyone deals with stressors in the same way. Some people are knocked quickly out of balance by stress, while others continue to be effortlessly active on various fronts, despite the stress they feel. Tiredness appears not to impact them.

In short, these people have a stress-bearing capacity that is much greater than the capacity of others. It takes longer before their balance between load and capacity loses its equilibrium. Once a state of imbalance is reached, they also generally have the ability to restore equilibrium much faster than others.

The manner in which you deal with stress is determined by a number of factors. Some people are naturally performance-oriented and demand a lot of themselves and others. They are always pushing their own boundaries, are often impatient and easily bored. They're the ones who are motivated first and foremost by a desire to see everything work better, faster and more efficiently. They seek success and to perform to the best of their ability, even when they don't have time pressure.

Others are seemingly less ambitious. They assess what is realistically achievable and set reasonable guidelines to reflect this. They are less obsessive, communicate better and know how to relax. These people often think in terms of problem solving and possess good analytical skills. When they're confronted with difficulties, they attempt to deal with them calmly, quickly assessing the scale and impact of the problem at hand, including a worst-case scenario. In many instances, this has a reassuring influence on those around them. This group of people is unquestionably more stress-resistant than the first group.

I have also noticed over the years that stress-resistant people often have an extensive social network. This means that they don't only share their problems with others, but can also push those problems into the background whenever the need arises. Success is also a factor in enhancing stress resistance. Often, successful people are stress-resistant people. But many wonder if they are stress-resistant because they are successful or successful because they are stress-resistant.

TAKE MATTERS INTO YOUR OWN HANDS!

The most effective tool to increase stress-resistance and mental resiliency is within your grasp. I mentioned earlier that it's not always possible to catch every wave and that if you wipe-out there are simple ways to find and ride another, for better and for longer.

The tool is: take good care of yourself. Get enough sleep, exercise sufficiently, eat and drink responsibly. This is the kind of Egopreneur you need to be: someone who makes time for themselves and looks after their most important asset – their own body.

Sleep, exercise and diet (nutrition) are the three essential pillars on which all my coaching trajectories are based. These three pillars, thanks to the better physical condition they generate, nearly always lead to a fourth pillar: greater mental resilience and, consequently, improved stress resistance.

Maybe it will surprise you, but if I was asked to put these pillars on a podium in order of priority, my gold medal would go to sleep, with exercise taking silver and diet taking bronze. Sleep has a huge impact on the way we function both mentally and physically – which is something else we'll look at in detail.

For me, exercise is (slightly) more important than diet, since research has shown that people who are overweight but take regular exercise and avoid sitting behind a desk all day are generally healthier than people who are not overweight but take hardly any extra exercise and remain glued to their computer for eight hours at a time. That being said, let's be perfectly clear: it is important to work at improving all three pillars, day after day after day!

THE SLEEP-EXERCISE-DIET PODIUM

An Egopreneur makes sure he gets
enough sleep, takes sufficient exercise,
and eats and drinks responsibly.

I referred above to the remarkable performance of the elite marathon runner, Eliud Kipchoge. There are a number of other things about him that I value and admire. For example, he claims that he never pushes himself over his limit when he is training. In fact, he seldom exceeds 80%. He saves the best of his strength and energy for race days. In this respect, the way to the top is clear and straightforward: it is simply a matter of working hard. You have to set the right priorities and do whatever is necessary to realise them. If you do this, you don't need shortcuts. Besides, shortcuts never work.

One of Kipchoge's favourite books (and also one of mine – see chapter 3) is *The Seven Habits of Highly Effective People* by Stephen R. Covey. Based on this and other books, the Kenyan has arrived at the following formula for success: motivation + discipline = consistency.

Above all, Eliud is convinced that there is a crucial connection between the body and the mind. 'It is not just about your legs,' he says, 'but also about your heart and your brain.' For him, pain is nothing more than a matter of perspective. If he is in pain, he banishes it by thinking of other things like the joy of crossing the finishing line, the pleasure he finds in running itself, etc.

Kipchoge epitomises the fact that phenomenal athletic achievements result from more than just training hard and pushing one's body beyond its limits. We can all learn from this: we must see all that we do and all that we are from a broader perspective, the perspective of the indisputable and unshakeable connection between body and mind.

6

Eight hours of sleep for everyone

The CEO of a medium-sized company told me during our first coaching session that her main problem was likely poor sleeping habits. Her sleeping patterns were irregular and she never stayed asleep for long. There were a number of reasons for this, she said: going to bed too late, (sometimes) too much alcohol before she went to bed, working too long and too late on the computer and too little movement and exercise during the day. In fact, she did just about everything that you should not do if you want to sleep well.

Unknown is unloved

A few years ago, I gave a lecture to a hundred or so top CEOs about the management of personal energy. I discussed at length the impact of sleep, diet and exercise on our physical and, above all, mental status. During the conversations I had after the lecture, it became clear that it was the information about sleep and the impact of a lack of it that had the biggest impression on my listeners.

Many of them seemed unaware of the negative impact of sleep deprivation on daily performance.

> The detrimental effects of
> sleeping less than six hours each
> night is hard to overestimate.

This didn't surprise me then and it doesn't surprise me now. For many people, not sleeping enough and functioning with relatively little sleep has become a kind of status symbol in recent years. I still regularly meet people who say: 'For me, four or five hours of sleep each night is enough. The next morning I am raring to go again.' I am afraid they are deceiving themselves. Years of research by the English scientist Matthew Walker, author of the bestseller *Why We Sleep*, has shown that everyone, without exception, needs seven to eight hours of sleep each night. People who think that four hours is enough have no idea how much better they would perform with two or three more hours of sleep.

A night with less than six hours of sleep has an immediate impact on both your mental and physical condition. What's more, a chronic shortage of sleep can significantly increase the risk of developing cancer, dementia, heart problems, strokes, type 2 diabetes and obesity. In addition, it reduces our natural resistance to infections and quickly impairs both your emotional and cognitive function. Every important organ in our body is affected by the amount we sleep.

As an Egopreneur in the making, it is therefore of great importance to take all steps possible to help you to develop positive sleep patterns. You must make sufficient time in your daily (and nightly) schedule to ensure that you always get your necessary seven or eight hours.

UPDATING OUR BRAINS

Perhaps the most important effect of sufficient sleep is on our brain functioning. During sleep, your brain is effectively cleansed during the two key phases of pattern: non-REM (rapid eye movement) and REM sleep.

During the non-REM phase, which generally takes place during the first part of the sleep cycle, all unnecessary and superfluous neural connections are eliminated. Our mental storage capacity is limited, so it is essential to remove redundant information to best prepare us for the next day. In other words, for your brain these early hours of sleep are like a 10 000 kilometre service for your car.

During the second phase of sleep, the REM phase, new neural connections are made. This ensures that newly learned information is fixed in the brain and that existing memories are straightened.

We need a minimum of seven hours of sleep for these two phases to be properly executed. Reducing the number of hours of sleep initially has an impact on our memory capacity. This explains, for example, why it's important for students to <u>not</u> get up early, not even on the day of their exams. Of course, revising what they've learned is also useful, providing it's after a good night's sleep.

A DIFFICULT CHILD

Our sleep patterns also have a clear effect on our rational behaviour and how we deal with emotions. One key part of our brain is the prefrontal cortex. To a large extent this part regulates the way the brain works. In fact, you can see it as a kind of brain-CEO. If your cerebral system is functioning properly, this part of the brain is able, up to a certain point, to keep stress and negative emotions under control.

However, if you're sleep deprived, the influence of the amygdala increases. This is the part of the brain that is responsible for the guidance and processing of emotions, such as fear. With too little sleep, we lose the ability to respond rationally to our emotions, we lose our neutrality and suddenly all our thoughts become emotionally charged. As a result, it becomes much harder to behave rationally, having profound consequences on our behaviour. This is the reason why a child who hasn't had enough sleep is difficult, if not impossible to manage. The lesson is clear: a healthy sleeping pattern is vitally important for optimal cognitive function.

Bearing this in mind, it is not unreasonable to question the value of the decisions taken by ministers after 24-hour meetings sometimes held during political negotiations or crises. Under the pressure of a deadline and racked by tiredness, they push through decisions that often turn out to be worthless. And there is little doubt that the politicians involved try to exploit the sleep deprivation of their political opponents to gain extra concessions. In a similar vein but in a completely different field, we can only hope that if you ever find yourself on an operating table, your surgeon has had a good night's sleep.

Sleeping well is especially important during periods of unusual stress. People who are under great stress or have had a traumatic experience are significantly less likely to be affected by PTSS (post-traumatic stress syndrome), depression and suicidal tendencies, providing they get enough sleep.

Citius, altius, fortius

Of course, it's not only our cognitive processes that are influenced by sleep. Sleep is also important for the body's recovery after physical effort. This physical recovery takes place primarily when we first fall asleep during non-REM sleep.

As long ago as 1980, the top Dutch cyclist Joop Zoetemelk commented: 'You win the Tour de France in bed.' Of course, there's more to it than that, but what Zoetemelk underlines is the importance of a good night's rest in achieving top physical performance. Even the now disgraced Lance Armstrong thought the same. He tried to keep his obligatory protocol and post-race duties to a strict minimum, so that he was able to get to bed an hour earlier than the other riders. In the course of a race that covers 21 stages, this means three days of additional sleep in comparison with his rivals. Of course, it later became clear that all this extra sleep was not the only reason for his seven Tour de France victories.

SLEEP COACH

Even so, the basic argument of Zoetemelk and Armstrong is valid. There is plenty of evidence to show that endurance – after less than seven to eight hours of sleep – during physical activity decreases significantly. The point at which exhaustion sets in lies between 10 and 30% earlier.

Other research examining the injury incidences of NBA basketball players over a full season concluded that the number of injuries declined considerably in relation to the players' hours of sleep: more sleep meant fewer injuries. The same study also revealed that players who slept for at least eight hours each night made 45% fewer fouls and lost the ball 37% less often.

Impact of sleep on sports

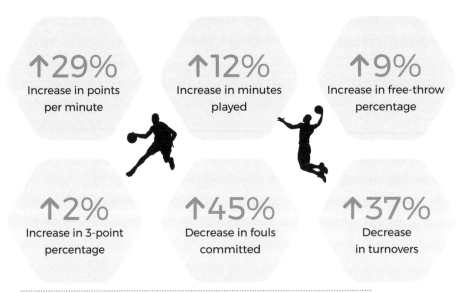

↑29%
Increase in points
per minute

↑12%
Increase in minutes
played

↑9%
Increase in free-throw
percentage

↑2%
Increase in 3-point
percentage

↑45%
Decrease in fouls
committed

↑37%
Decrease
in turnovers

THE IMPACT OF SLEEP ON SPORTING PERFORMANCE IN THE NBA

(Source: Matthew Walker, *Why we sleep*, 2017.)

How simple can the life of a coach be! Just make sure that your athletes get sufficient sleep and the positive impact on their performance will be enormous, much greater than the impact of any training. If, in addition, you also understand that sleep has a similarly positive influence on the motoric learning process, it becomes as clear as the eyes can see that it's in the best interest of every serious athlete to optimise their pattern of sleep, with a minimum of eight hours per night as their guideline.

Bearing this in mind, it's strange, then, that in sports like football so many players (often with the approval of their trainers) spend their free days and sometimes even the night after a game in discotheques! When the German football club Fortuna Düsseldorf lost match after match in 2016, the owner of a well-known local disco, Ruas Studios, imposed a ban on all the team's players. He simply wouldn't let them in anymore. Did the ban have an impact on the team's results? I have no idea, but it's clear that the owner thought it would.

Staying awake during the day

Do you find it difficult to sleep at night and stay awake during the day? It sounds like a strange combination, but it is far from uncommon. Coffee often plays a crucial role in this process. Surveys of the audiences at my lectures on energy management regularly reveal that many people drink more than five cups of coffee a day, and sometimes a great deal more. In part, it's habit. But usually the larger part is to combat tiredness and overcome energy dips.

The stimulant in coffee is caffeine. To understand its effect, you first need to be aware of the existence of adenosine, a substance in the brain that increases our urge to sleep. If we sleep for seven or eight hours, the concentration of adenosine at the start of each new day is low. As the day progresses, its concentration gradually increases, and so does the urge to sleep. By the time late evening comes, the level of adenosine in our system means that this urge has become a strong one, and we are ready to go to bed. If, however, we fail to get seven or eight hours of sleep, the concentration of adenosine becomes too high too early in the day. We want to go to sleep but we can't – and this is where coffee comes in. The caffeine in coffee neutralises the effect of the adenosine by blocking its receptors in the brain. This means that your urge to sleep diminishes and you suddenly feel more alert.

'What's wrong with that?' you might say. Unfortunately, there is a catch. The half-life of caffeine, which is the time it takes for half of the substance to work its way out of your system, is roughly six hours. This means that if you drink coffee in the late afternoon, you will still be feeling its invigorating effects until late in the evening, by which time you will usually be trying to go to sleep and potentially failing.

Many people have a bad night, because not only do they drink too much coffee, but also too late in the day. This vicious circle becomes difficult to break: sleeping poorly – tired during the day – too much coffee – sleeping poorly…

Apart from its interaction with adenosine, caffeine is also an approved stimulant in elite sports with a positive effect on an athlete's endurance. The standard dose is 3 to 4 milligrams per kilogram of body weight. An athlete weighing 70 kilograms should therefore take between 250-300 grams of caffeine roughly half an hour before the event.

The impact of caffeine on our fine motor skills is less clear cut. Interesting in this respect is a study carried out in 1982 on behalf of NASA by David A. Noever and his colleagues at Princeton University. Spiders that had been dosed with LSD, ecstasy, marijuana, chloral hydrate (a sedative used by people with epilepsy) and caffeine were monitored to see what effect it would have on the spinning of their webs. The following diagram depicts the fascinating results. It can be seen that the webs of 'drugged' spiders differed dramatically from the norm, including the web of the spider under the influence of caffeine.

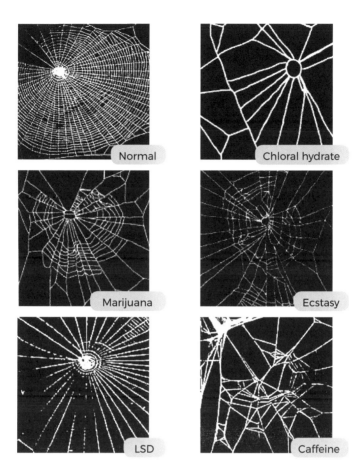

THE IMPACT OF CAFFEINE AND OTHER SUBSTANCES ON THE SPINNING OF SPIDER WEBS

(Source: Peter Witt, 'Spider Webs and Drugs.' Scientific American (1954), Vol.191(6).)

Like coffee, drinking alcohol before you go to sleep is not a good idea. Alcohol has a sedating effect, which perhaps gives you the feeling that you can drop off to sleep more easily. However, alcohol actually ensures that your sleep is restless and fragmented, with a particularly negative impact on your REM sleep. Because REM sleep is also important for memory function, it explains why people who drink a lot of alcohol so often have problems remembering things.

The excessive use of alcohol is a seriously underestimated problem. Some time ago, I was involved in a curious discussion with a number of business leaders, who saw no problem with drinking a number of glasses of wine each day, primarily in the evening. They were prepared to sacrifice most things to achieve a healthier lifestyle, but not that! For them a few glasses of good wine was compensation for all their hard work and the stress they had experienced during the day. And, of course, they are not alone in this. Many people end up with an alcohol dependence almost before they know it. The impact on their daily functioning is immense, especially in regard to memory, ability to control emotions, creativity, objectivity and linear thinking.

> Excessive use of
> alcohol has more effect
> on our daily functioning
> than we can imagine.

The recommendation by the World Health Organisation (WHO) is crystal clear: everyone should limit themselves to no more than 10 units of alcohol each week (a unit being one 25 cl glass of beer or one 10 cl glass of wine). What's more, it's also important to have a number of completely 'alcohol-free' days in the course of the week.

THE SCREEN

In addition to adenosine, your body also contains a second substance that helps to make you feel sleepy: melatonin. This hormone is secreted by the pineal gland and is sometimes known as the vampire hormone or the night hormone, because the level of secretion increases in the dark.

Contrary to popular belief, melatonin has no direct influence on the sleeping process itself. But it does let the body know when darkness is falling, indicating that it's time to go to sleep.

Production of melatonin (pg/ml)

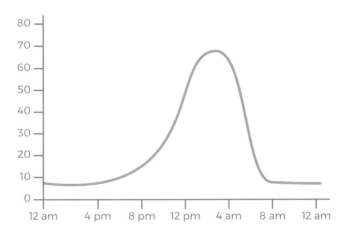

THE MELATONIN CYCLE

The screens of computers and tablets emit blue light, which has the same effect on your body as daylight. This means that if you work with such a screen late into the evening, your body will still think it's daytime – resulting in suppressed melatonin production. You'll find it much harder to get to sleep when you finally do stop working. You have delayed your sleep process kick-starter by the number of hours you've been sitting at your computer or tablet. For this reason, it's important to stop looking at a screen at least two hours before you plan to go to bed, and preferably earlier.

Strength through sleep

Today, we have monophasic sleep patterns. We sleep just once every 24 hours; namely, at night, when it is dark. However, that hasn't always been the case. In fact, biologically, we humans have a natural biphasic sleep pattern, which means that each of us, to a greater or lesser degree, are subject to a midday 'dip'.

This midday dip can be enhanced by a heavy lunch. Your stomach is a muscle, so that if you have eaten too much the body diverts extra blood to assist the digestive process. This reduces the amount of blood transported to the brain, decreasing your level of alertness. It means that the worst moment for intellectual and physical performance is shortly after lunch. So, don't give a presentation that starts at 2 o'clock in the afternoon: most of your listeners won't be feeling up to it!

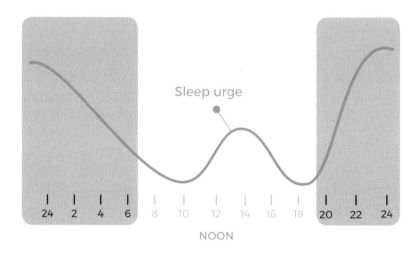

THE BIPHASIC SLEEP PATTERN

People made the switch from a biphasic to a monophasic pattern of sleep during the transition from an agrarian to an industrial society. Industrial production processes are continuous, so it was no longer possible to take an early afternoon nap. This was, however, feasible in the agricultural era, when nearly everyone settled down for forty-winks after their midday meal. The present day siesta, mainly in southern countries, is a last vestige of this phenomenon.

THE POWER NAP

Today, there is renewed interest in the idea of a siesta in other parts of the world and with good reason. This southern custom has been transformed and also given a new name: the power nap. The power nap doesn't last as long as a siesta, 20 to maximum 30 minutes is sufficient. If you sleep for any longer, there is a chance that you'll fall into a deep sleep, from which you will find it hard to emerge without continuing to feel drowsy. Deep sleep during the day also has a negative influence on your sleep at night.

A power nap has a
huge positive impact on your cognitive
and physical functioning.

In particular, a power nap can be extremely useful if you have not slept well the previous night. It allows you to 'catch up' on your lost sleep and helps to offset the effects of your bad night, at least in part. But even if you don't need to play catch up, taking a nap after lunch is beneficial in more ways than one. Research has shown that taking a power nap increases memory test performance, lowers risk of suffering from heart problems, and supports growing old in a healthy way.

Bart, one of my coachees, regularly takes a power nap in the run-up to his TV broadcasts. He says that he feels much more alert afterward and that the questions he has prepared with his editorial team are more firmly fixed in his mind.

I also advise my athletes to have a short sleep after they have completed their daily training, since this helps them to better recover from their efforts.

Today, the positive impact of the power nap is widely recognised in the business world. Companies like Nike, Google, Zappos, Cisco and Procter & Gamble have all provided power nap rooms for their employees. So who's next?

> Back to the CEO with the sleepless nights:
>
> After taking a few elementary measures, her sleep pattern gradually began to improve. Until one day she said to me: 'The biggest change I've noticed is that I can now read a book again and still remember what I read on the previous page!'

Tips

» Dim the lights in your house in good time during the evening.

» Develop a fixed and relaxing sleep ritual. Take a warm bath, read a book, listen to music, always go to bed at the same time, etc. Also try to get up at the same time each morning.

» Ensure good sleep hygiene: a firm mattress, a cool room temperature, sufficient darkness and no disturbing noise.

» Avoid heavy meals late in the evening.

» Limit alcohol consumption to a maximum of one unit per evening.

» Limit coffee consumption to a maximum of three cups per day and drink the last cup around midday.

» Take exercise every day, preferably during the morning.

» Avoid screen use (computer, tablet, smartphone) during the last three hours before you go to bed.

» Avoid heavy physical effort during the final hours before you go to bed.

» Avoid heavy intellectual effort in the final hours before you go to bed. Write down the things you need to do urgently next day, so that you don't need to worry about them once you are between the sheets.

» If you can't get to sleep or if you are awake for more than half an hour in the middle of the night, get up. Do something restful, like reading, until you feel sleepy again, then go back to bed.

7 Improving performance through more exercise

Christophe has a leading position in a multinational company, with responsibility for Central Europe and the Balkans. He is very busy, every week visiting a number of the countries under his charge. Christophe is also a very keen athlete. He runs marathons frequently and takes on serious cycling challenges. He's almost always in top condition, notwithstanding his highly demanding job.

Know the reason why

'Who makes resolutions at the start of each new year?' Whenever I ask this question in my lectures, almost everyone raises their hand. But when I ask 'And who manages to keep them?', most hands lower.

This informal survey more or less matches the results of scientific research, showing that 70% of those with positive new year's resolutions, like adopting a healthier lifestyle and taking more exercise, have given up their plans by the end of March. And the other 30%? Some of them manage to keep going until the end of the year, but many others fall by the wayside between April and December.

This was also reflected in a study by the University of Antwerp in 2014 on participation in the Antwerp 10 Miles. 70% of the runners who took part in the event for the first time stopped running permanently after they crossed the finishing line. Odd, isn't it?

To explain this, we need to look again at the golden circles of Simon Sinek, first shown in chapter 3 when we learned the importance of asking 'why'. In Sinek's vision, you can only be successful if you base your actions on the inner circle, on the why, on your own vision, mission and values that motivate you. Success can only be achieved if you understand why you do what you do. Let's apply this theory to the participants in the Antwerp race.

Most of them took 'what' as their starting point: the 10 Miles. They took part simply to take part, without having any deeper motive. Perhaps they had seen the great atmosphere that surrounds the event each year, or an enthusiastic neighbour had encouraged them to try it, or perhaps they were just curious to see what it was like to participate in such a fun event.

Having decided on what they would do, the Antwerp race participants moved onto the 'how', on where to begin. In Belgium, where I live, there are plenty of options for people who want to get started in amateur running competitions:

download the 'Start 2 Run' application by the Flemish radio presenter Evy Gruyaert. Buy a book with training programmes, find similar programmes online, join the local athletics club, ask the advice of an experienced running coach, etc. Once they find how to get started, they train until the big race day finally arrives. When they cross the finishing line it's 'mission accomplished', having achieved what they set out to achieve. So, why would they keep bettering their physical fitness? In 70% of cases, for no reason at all.

Let's now look at things from the other side of the spectrum, starting with Sinek's inner circle and the 'why'. If you ask yourself why you want to start running, the process leading up to race day unfolds very differently... Imagine that you're not happy with the way things are going in your life. You are feeling stressed, both at work and at home. You are not sleeping well and you are carrying more weight than you should. A routine visit to the doctor makes clear that you need to do something about your physical fitness. Something has to change. In other words, your 'why' is obvious.

This brings you to the second circle: how can you do something about your problem? Once again, there are plenty of options: ask for the help of a psychologist, practice mindfulness, seek dietary advice from a nutritional specialist, join the local fitness club, buy a bike, or perhaps start jogging. Let's imagine you choose this final option. Now you've opened yourself to the same range of choices as the race participant discussed above, who started from Sinek's outer circle.

Now imagine that you've begun your training programme and you soon feel better. Your stress is more under control, you're losing weight, your blood pressure and cholesterol levels are down. Overall, you feel that you are on the way to achieving your why – your reason for running in the first place. Finally, you feel ready for your first race. You register, you run and you cross the finish line. Will you stop running? Of course not! You didn't decide to start running just for that one race, but to get healthy, more fit and resilient. The race was just one part of a trajectory that is by no means finished. Instead you will continue running with élan! The moral of the story: make sure you know the reason you want to run.

To be healthy, you
don't really need to do sport.
Just ensuring sufficient
physical activity each day is enough.

When people are advised to exercise more, they are often frightened off by the idea. They associate exercise with running marathons or cycling up a mountain and exceeding their physical limits to the point of exhaustion. Let me put your mind at rest. This is not the way it has to be. If health, rather than performance, is your priority, you really don't need to take up sport at all. All you need to do is to make sure that you engage in sufficient physical activity, every day. Of course, sport is also physical activity, but physical activity doesn't necessarily have to be sport.

COUGHING LESS

Evidence for the importance of daily exercise is overwhelming. Physical activity is good for your muscles and bones, improving heart function, blood circulation, and immune system strength. Regular exercise reduces the risk of certain cancers, strokes and other medical conditions, such as diabetes and osteoporosis.

Exercise can even help you to fight influenza. People who regularly engage in physical activity are much less susceptible to viral infections of the upper respiratory tract. As depicted in the following figure, even moderate exercise is of great benefit. But as the graph shows, you must know the risks of overdoing it. The likelihood of succumbing to a respiratory virus is actually increased because over-exercising can weaken your immune system.

Risk of viral infections in the upper airways

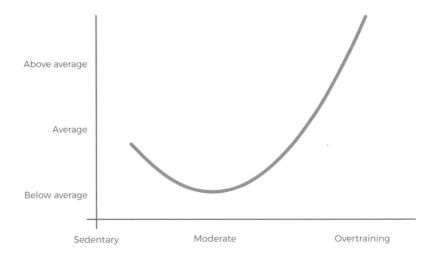

....

**THE RISK OF VIRAL INFECTIONS IN THE UPPER AIRWAYS IN
RELATION TO TRAINING INTENSITY**

(Source: D.C. Nieman, Appalachian State University, 1997.)

EXERCISE: NOT A MIRACLE RECIPE
FOR LOSING WEIGHT

Exercise burns fat. But if you are hoping that more exercise will help you to lose
weight, I am afraid that you are likely to be disappointed. The reason for this is
actually quite simple.

To shed one kilogram of fat, you need to burn between 7000 and 8000 kilocalories. During an hour of relaxed running, depending on your weight and the
pace you set, you use an average of 500 to 600 kilocalories. In other words, to
burn off one kilogram of fat you will need to run for between 12 and 15 hours!

And this is assuming that you don't put back any of the calories you use up during your run.

Essentially, you would need to be a very dedicated runner to start seeing a downward trend on your scales. What's more, even if you do lose some of your fat as a result of running, you will build up your muscle mass in parallel. Muscle is denser than fat, and weighs more on a volume by volume basis. As a result, running may make you look slimmer as your muscles strengthen, but you won't necessarily weigh less. In fact, in some cases you may even weigh more due to an increase in muscle mass.

That's why some athletes find it so difficult to achieve their best competition weight. No matter how many hours they train, they not only burn fat, but also sugars, especially when the training is intense. What's more, after each training they also need to replenish their energy reserves, so that they can train again with equal intensity the next day or start a race with a full fuel tank.

But it's not all bad news. Exercise contributes indirectly towards weight control. I have seen on many occasions how making a conscious attempt to exercise more, goes hand in hand with a generally healthier lifestyle – bettering one's diet and pattern of sleep. Combining these actions is the best way to lose weight.

MENS SANA IN CORPORE SANO

Exercise not only makes your body fitter and healthier. It also improves your mental faculties. *Mens sana in corpore sano,* 'a healthy mind in a healthy body', is an aphorism attributed to the Latin poet Juvenal writing in the 2nd century AD. In 1898, the German psychiatrist Emil Kraepelin also recommended people to engage in sport, because he believed it not only increased physical strength but also a person's decision-making powers.

Scientific evidence to confirm that exercise in all its forms offers both physical and psychological benefits is well recorded, but was given a new impetus in the mid-1970s. In 1974, Dr Thaddeus Kostrubala, head of the psychiatric department at the Mercy Hospital in San Diego, California, began a series of experiments with students from the nearby San Diego University. He evaluated the physiological and psychological advantages of prolonged exercise, such as running and walking. The results were so positive that he decided to develop Running Therapy for his patients, a therapy he described in detail in his book *The Joy of Running*.

This represented a significant deviation from classic therapy. Patients who followed the new approach combined an hour of group therapy with two to four hours of running or walking each week, with at least one training session in the company of a therapist. During these sessions, considerable attention was devoted to the awareness of bodily sensations.

The results of the new therapy were spectacular. The heart rate of people suffering from depression as a consequence of problems at home or at work, or by some other psychological condition, was significantly lower, both when resting and active. They burned fat at a higher rate and their blood pressure and cholesterol levels fell. At the same time, their feelings of fear decreased, while their sense of well-being and self-esteem grew. They had more control over their daily stressors and an increased tolerance of them.

Subsequent research has confirmed these results. Running therapy is effective in treating depression and helping people with symptoms of burn-out. In fact, in many cases running and distance walking were as effective, if not more effective, than the use of medication.

Nowadays, exercise therapy is widely used in psychiatric health care. For example, a protocol based on the therapy has been launched with success at the Public Psychiatric Care Centre in the Flemish town of Geel. Many patients testify to the positive effect of sport and exercise on their mental well-being.

CALM THROUGH ACTION

In order to understand why exercise therapy and exercise in general has such a positive impact on our brain, we must return to the 'fight or flight' mechanism discussed in chapter 5.

In the distant past, survival was often difficult for our ancestors. For example, finding enough food was often a life-threatening business. Competition was fierce and predators were everywhere. In these circumstances, it was frequently necessary to decide what action to take: fight or flight. This decision and the subsequent action were preceded by the release of stress hormones, resulting in a heart rate, breathing and body temperature shooting up rapidly. This allowed people to deal with the dangerous situations they faced. After the fight or flight had taken place, the impact of the stress hormones decreased again, resulting in a new state of calm.

> Additional exercise reduces
> the impact of your stress hormones,
> so that you become calmer.

Physiologically, we are not different from our ancestors, but our stressors and how we react to them have changed. A new deadline or target, an unexpected e-mail, problems with your colleagues or your boss are potentially threatening situations. Like your ancestors, they increase the concentrations of stress hormones in our blood. But today you take no further action. You don't throw your computer out of the window. You don't run screaming from the office. You don't punch your colleague on the nose (a good thing, too!). In short, there is no fight or flight. However, stress hormones are released into circulation regardless. By the time you get home at the end of the day your stress levels are through the roof. Exhausted, you crash into bed and fall asleep within minutes, only to wake up two hours later with the same problems and negative thoughts racing through your mind. Once awake, you may lie there worrying until morning.

This is why additional exercise helps budding Egopreneurs reduce the impact of stress hormones and rediscover your inner calm. Because when you exercise, you actually copy your ancestors from all those centuries ago. Exercise is the modern-day version of fight or flight.

A HIGH WITHOUT DRUGS

There is a second reason why exercise is good for your brain and, once again, we find the explanation in our ancestors. Back in primeval times, people travelled for days on end to find food for the group. Ignoring their increasing exhaustion, they would press on, refusing to return to their tribe until they had found suffi-cient food to ensure everyone's survival. They were able to persevere because the brain releases endorphins into their system in response to exertion. Endor-phins are a morphine-like substance produced by the body to ease pain during excessive physical exertion, making it bearable. In short, it is a kind of internal drug. These same endorphins make it possible for top athletes to go the extra mile, time after time, even after hard periods of training. Endorphins also give runners an almost euphoric feeling, known as 'runner's high'. This is something that happens particularly amongst well-trained long-distance runners. Some of them say that everything seems clearer when they are running and that after a while they lose all sense of time. After, they often can't even remember the route they followed.

HAPPINESS FOR THE TAKING

One of the consequences of this endorphin release is that sport, over time, can become addictive. Have you never noticed how novice runners and cyclists want to run and cycle more and more, to the point that they can no longer contemplate a life without it?

This addiction is psychological and physical. In time, the body adapts to a high level of exertion and the endorphins it generates. When an athlete is unable to practice their sport for a long period, due to injury for example, they fall prey to all kinds of medical complaints, such as heart palpitations. This explains, for example, why professional cyclists are advised to incorporate a withdrawal period when they leave competition. It's not good for them to suddenly stop training. Instead, they should reduce frequency and intensity – slowly.

Exercise makes you happier.

Scientific research has also revealed that physical activity stimulates the release of serotonin in the brain. Serotonin is known as the 'happiness hormone' and has a beneficial effect on, amongst other things, our memory, self-confidence, moods and emotions.

It couldn't be any clearer. Exercise has a major positive impact on your brain. In short, it makes you happier.

SMARTER

There are numerous indications that moderately intense exercise has positive effects on memory. For example, in 2016 Miriam S. Nokia and her colleagues at the University of Jyväskylä (Finland) published the findings on the impact of physical activity on neuronal growth in the hippocampi of rats. They investigated the impact of physical activity on the creation of new nerve connections in the rats' brains; more particularly in the hippocampus (the part of the brain that is important for memory function).

A first group of rats was required to power train. They had to repeatedly climb up a slope with a weight attached to their tails. A second group needed to run at a moderate pace on a treadmill. A third group performed so-called high intensity interval training (HIIT), where the pace of the treadmill varied from relatively slow to fast.

After a number of weeks, the researchers noted a significant increase in the number of nerve connections in the hippocampi of the rats that had undertaken the moderately paced training on the treadmill. No change was noted in the other two groups.

EXERCISING TO SLEEP BETTER

Physical exercise can also have a significant impact on sleep patterns. In this, various factors play a role.

Your most important stress hormone is cortisol. If you're under stress, the level of cortisol in your blood increases. If you feel relaxed, your level of cortisol decreases. Physical exercise, and particularly its intensity, has a marked influence on this level. Intensive exercise leads to a heightened level of cortisol. Gentle exercise, such as walking, leads to a reduced level.

If you want a good night's rest, stress should of course be kept to a minimum and intense physical effort should be avoided in the hours immediately before you go to bed. In contrast, taking a quiet walk during these final hours can only help you to sleep better.

MORE SELF-CONFIDENCE

In 2016, I became an adviser to the then Minister of Education, Hilde Crevits (CD&V), for the Flanders region in Belgium. She asked me to devise a plan that encourages physical exercise in children during school hours. The large majority of school children in Flanders fail to meet the recommended level of one hour daily of moderate to intense physical activity such as jogging, dancing, cycling, skateboarding, playing sports in a club, etc. In fact, in the 10-17-year age group less than a third meet this norm!

My plan proposed that children in primary education in Flanders (2,342 schools) should be encouraged to exercise for 15 extra minutes each day during or between lessons. If we equate these 15 minutes of physical activity with covering a distance of 1.6 kilometres (analogous with the Daily Mile, an international initiative that encourages pupils to jog or run one mile each day during school hours), this would mean that Flemish children would cover 150,000,000 cumulative kilometres over the course of a school year. That is the distance between our planet and the sun. For that reason, I named this daily exercise 'Sun Time'. The teachers were free to use the 15 minutes as they saw fit, as long as the children were kept constantly active and in motion.

The plan looked good on paper. There is ample research demonstrating that children who get sufficient exercise are healthier, more attentive and calmer (both at school and at home). They also concentrate better and achieve better school results.

At the request of Minister Crevits, the Faculty of Movement and Rehabilitation Sciences at KU Leuven studied the effects of the Sun Time programme. They concluded that the children covered more distance during the allotted time than at the outset of the programme and their school work improved. But that was not all. Children with low self-esteem also seemed to gain in self-confidence and became more satisfied with their own appearance. In other words, taking up more exercise each day helps children in many ways.

Despite these results, many teachers weren't convinced to take part in the project. In fact, only 10% of schools registered to participate. If everything had gone according to the provisions of the plan, by now Flemish children would have covered twice the distance to the sun. At it is, they have only covered a third of the distance. One of the most frequent comments to justify non-participation was: 'As long as the minister fails to make additional time, resources and staff available, we don't feel able to take on this extra commitment.' What additional time? The plan foresees that the exercise should take place during the normal lesson schedule. What additional resources? The 15 minutes of physical activity costs nothing. What extra staff? The exercise is monitored by the existing teaching staff.

The real problem is that we have a school culture focused too much on intelligence and acquisition of knowledge and too little on the proper care of the body. Sadly, there is no exercise culture in our schools. I continually find this hard to understand. What could be better than encouraging all children to become fitter and to give vulnerable children a heightened feeling of self? Why is there so much resistance to helping children find the road to Egopreneurship from an early age?

How and what

By now, it should be clear that you need to make a serious effort if you want to become healthier. The World Health Organisation (WHO) recommends that each week we should undertake five 30-minute periods of 'moderately intense' exercise and three 20-minute periods of 'intense' exercise. 'Moderately intense' exercise means things like running your errands by bike or on foot, or working in the garden.

'Intense exercise' increases your heart rate and breathing rhythm. This means walking or cycling at a faster than normal pace, light jogging, etc. It does not mean that you have to practice 'sport' in a way that leaves you out of breath. As we've seen, intense activity increases the level of the stress hormone cortisol in your blood, whereas light exercise causes that level to fall.

KEEP IT SIMPLE

It is possible (and acceptable) to keep things simple. Just taking the required number of steps per day will give a serious health boost. Today, 10 000 steps is a popular figure and is used by many as a daily objective. On average, we take between 4000 and 6000 steps daily. For those with a sedentary job, this falls to between 2000 and 3000 steps. To reach the 10 000 figure, this means you need to walk roughly an extra half hour on top of your normal daily activity. That's quite a lot, but you don't need to do it all in one go. There are plenty of things you can do during the day to help you. Take the stairs instead of the lift, make short journeys on foot, go for a short walk during your lunch break, etc. You will get there!

Another easier option, which has more or less the same positive effect as 10 000 steps, is to plan three ten-minute walks at above normal pace into your daily schedule. For example, you can do this once in the morning, once at lunchtime and once in the afternoon. Surely this is something that all of us should be able to arrange?

An excellent aid to help you to count your daily steps is a wearable step counter. This simple device often seems to work wonders for the people who use it, primarily because it provides them with continuous feedback about their stepping performance. A simple glance at the screen tells you how many steps you have done and how many you have still got to do. And once you have reached your target, you are awarded points for your effort!

> Walking at a good pace for three ten-minute periods each day will bring you a long way.

It is a good idea to buy a step counter that can be synchronised with your smartphone. This allows you to record your daily steps over a longer period. The more sophisticated counters also give feedback about calories burned and your sleep pattern. Some can even monitor your stress levels throughout the day.

SOMETHING A BIT MORE TESTING?

For people who want something more challenging, but without seriously 'training', engaging in a more intense form of exercise for 30 minutes three times a week is a good place to start. This might include jogging, swimming lengths at the local pool, cycling or cardio-training (rowing, stepping, cross training, etc.).

Once again, it is not necessary to make your exercise 'hurt'. You should feel it a little in your muscles, your heart rate should increase and your body temperature should rise, but that's all. There is no need for you to lose your breath. However, it's important to remember that these three periods of activity are additional; you must also continue to take sufficient low-intensity exercise each day.

Of course, it's not a problem if you want to get your exercise by actively participating in sport. Many people like, or need, the challenge this presents and are stimulated by the idea of achieving a good level of performance in a demanding setting. Sport training results in greater general and cardio-vascular fitness than exercise taken purely for health purposes.

As an added bonus, practising a sport can also strengthen your network as an Egopreneur. I have got to know many people by cycling with them. Many business deals are concluded on a bike now instead of a golf course. Even so, it needs to be repeated: taking part in sport in this intense manner is not necessary if all you are interested in is improving your general health and mental resilience.

SITTING IS THE NEW SMOKING

A crucial factor that we have not yet mentioned is the importance of breaking your sitting pattern. In a relatively short period of time, we humans have changed from being physically active on our feet for most of the day to creatures who now spend most of the day sitting. In fact, many of us spend more than ten hours each day in a seated position at work, in the car, lounging at home in an armchair, etc.

We have become so sedentary that sitting is described as the new smoking. Research has shown that there is a significant correlation between the amount of time we spend sitting and the likelihood of avoiding medical conditions like cancer, cardio-vascular disease and diabetes. Put simply, the effect of continuous sitting on our health is disastrous.

For this reason, it's recommended not to remain sitting for uninterrupted periods of more than one hour. Make sure that you get up regularly out of your chair. Conduct meetings in a standing position. Do the same during your coffee breaks. These are all useful ways to break up your sitting pattern. This is another area where your step counter can help you. Most models also remind you when it's time to stand up for a few minutes.

Be aware that you can satisfy all the other exercise norms we have discussed above, but still be affected by the negative consequences of too much sitting. It is not enough simply to do your 10 000 steps or your 30 minutes of walking each day. This is not an either/or scenario. It is an and/and scenario. In addition to sufficient exercise, you also need to improve your sitting pattern. The human frame was designed for movement, not for sitting on your backside. So, move it!

When I asked Christophe how he manages to combine a busy professional life with making enough time to train, he showed me his daily planner. For every day, without fail, there was an entry that read 'me time'. He sees these periods as sacred and uses the time exclusively for himself, nearly always for training. His meetings and other appointments are made with this 'me time' in mind, not the other way around. For him, this is a question of priorities – and the highest priority is some time for himself, like a true Egopreneur!

Tips

» Make use of every opportunity to increase your daily number of steps.
  - Always use the stairs.
  - If you are early for an appointment, go for a short walk while you are waiting.
  - Park your car a few hundred metres from the place of your appointment.
  - Go for a walk during part of your lunch break.
  - Go to the shops on foot.

» Plan three ten-minute walks into your agenda each day.

» Conduct face-to-face conversations while walking.

» Buy a step counter and aim to walk a minimum of 7,500 steps each day (preferably 10,000).

» Keep three one-hour periods free in your agenda each week, during which you can exercise a little more intensely for 20 to 30 minutes without stress. Never compromise on this 'me time'.

» Break your sitting pattern at least once every hour.

» Take your coffee breaks standing up.

» Conduct meetings in a standing position.

8

Eat, don't diet!

I was introduced to Jan in 2017, a young sixty-something with a busy and high-stress life. Like many others, he was focused 100% on his work managing the various branches of his catering business. This took up nearly all his time, from first thing in the morning until last thing at night. His medical report was far from good. He was overweight, with high blood pressure and cholesterol. He slept badly and drank more than ten cups of coffee each day, most of them offered to him during branch visits. And not just coffee: it was usually coffee with a biscuit or chocolate! 'I often feel so tired,' he told me.

Being overweight uses up a great deal of energy. A few years ago, I did a simple test. I walked on a treadmill for a fixed period at a pace of 6 kilometres per hour. My heart rate fluctuated around 100 beats per minute. I then repeated the test, but this time carrying a 3-kilogram weight in each hand. My heart rate immediately increased by 10 to 15 beats per minute.

The impact of being overweight on the body's locomotor system is huge. When you run, the impact on your knees, for example, is three times your body weight (depending on the speed you run). If you weigh 70 kilograms, this means that the strain on your knees is 210 kilograms. If you weigh 100 kilograms, this strain shoots up to 300 kilograms – which means a world of difference for your poor bones and joints.

Eating less also has other beneficial consequences, although they are perhaps less obvious. Research has shown that a reduced calorie intake can lead to better results in memory tests. The explanation for this is connected to our evolutionary past: the scarcity of food made our ancestors extra alert, so that they could seize every opportunity to find enough to survive.

In other words, there are reasons other than your health to keep your body weight at a correct level.

> Exercise alone will not
> help you to lose weight
> in a sustainable manner.

If you want to lose weight and keep it off, there is little to be gained from exercising to excess or from eating low-fat snacks between meals. I know from many years of experience that strictly limiting your number of calories seldom or never results in lasting weight loss. I know too that eating a lot of simple sugars is unhealthy and that sugars can cause intestinal imbalance and disrupt your intestinal flora. This is important, because research recently carried out by scientists of the Flemish Intestinal Flora Project demonstrated that there is a link between the condition of the flora and depression. Good intestinal functioning is therefore crucial for our general physical and mental health.

I am not a dietary expert and have no intention of giving you detailed advice on healthy eating. I will therefore confine myself, as I do with my coachees, to explaining a number of the key physiological principles and their consequences. Once my coachees have understood these things, they're usually capable of successfully adjusting their own daily diets to make them healthier.

Avoid simple sugars, go for complex carbohydrates

When you read the list of products on food packaging, you'll see a distinction between carbohydrates and sugars. The sugars mentioned are actually simple carbohydrates. The carbohydrates mentioned are complex carbohydrates, made up from chains of simple carbohydrates.

The sugars are found in foodstuff like sweets, cakes, biscuits, chocolate, jam, soft drinks and fruit. Complex carbohydrates are found in bread, vegetables, nuts, potatoes, cereals, rice and pasta.

An important difference between the two is that sugars are absorbed very quickly into the blood, whereas carbohydrates first need to be broken down before they can enter the bloodstream. This latter process takes more time. As a result of their more rapid absorption, simple sugars are also referred to as fast sugars.

It is vital that the sugar level (also known as the glucose level) in the blood remains within strictly defined lower and upper limits. Too little sugar in your blood makes you feel tired and listless and in extreme cases can even lead to a loss of consciousness and coma. Too much sugar is even more harmful and is now generally seen as a silent killer. It significantly increases the likelihood of cardio-vascular disease and dementia, causing the accelerated ageing of all your bodily tissues. This explains why it's important for people with diabetes to constantly monitor their sugar level and keep it under control through the use of medication such as insulin.

The following diagram shows what happens when you absorb simple carbohydrates or sugars.

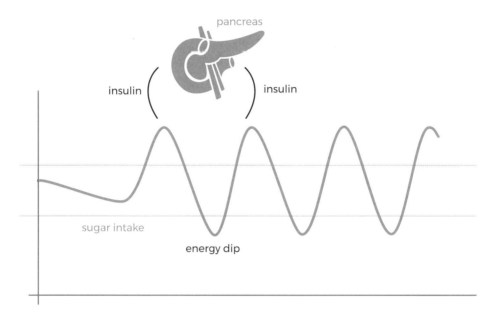

....

THE IMPACT OF SIMPLE SUGARS ON THE BLOOD SUGAR LEVEL AND INSULIN PRODUCTION

The sugar that you eat is taken quickly into the blood, so that your sugar level rises above the maximum level of tolerance. This sends an alarm signal to your body, so that your pancreas immediately secretes insulin to bring the sugar level back down to an acceptable level. The excess sugar is transported to the liver and to your fat cells, where it is converted into body fat.

In other words, the insulin reaction forces down the sugar level, often to below its normal level. When this happens, there is a shortage of sugar in your blood, which can lead to an energy dip. You feel tired and lethargic. What's more, you also feel hungry. So what do you do? You almost automatically reach for a new sugar-rich snack, which simply repeats the process. More and more sugar is successively transported to the fat cells, resulting ultimately in being overweight or obese.

People who eat too much sugar, who have repeated insulin spikes in their blood, eventually become insulin-resistant and will develop type 2 diabetes. If these people do nothing to change their dietary habits and lifestyle, which essentially means eating more low-sugar food and exercising more, they will become gradually dependent on medication to keep their insulin level under control.

In contrast, complex carbohydrates are absorbed more slowly into the blood, because they first need to be broken down. As a result, they generate comparatively lower sugar spikes and have a lesser effect on insulin release. So the message is clear: opt to include complex carbohydrates in your diet, and preferably the ones that are high in fibres, like wholemeal bread, wholemeal breakfast cereals, wholemeal pasta and brown rice.

You have probably noticed that fruit also contains an abundance of sugar. But isn't fruit supposed to be healthy? Yes, but the important thing is how you consume it. If you drink freshly pressed fruit juice, you are actually drinking a glass full of simple sugars, which will stimulate the large-scale counter-production of insulin. A glass of fruit juice contains the equivalent of seven lumps of sugar, which is roughly the same as a glass of some other sweet soft drink. In other words (and contrary to what many people think), fruit juice is <u>not</u> healthy. In contrast, eating pieces of fruit is healthy. An apple, for example, contains high concentrations of fibres, indigestible materials that slow down the digestive process. As a result, the apple's sugars are released much more gradually into the bloodstream, avoiding the potential negative consequences. Conclusion: eat two or three pieces of fruit per day, but steer well clear of fruit juice.

TIMING IS EVERYTHING

Many dietary experts say that it is a good idea to eat a number of (low-fat) snacks throughout the day. The main reason for this advice is that it repeatedly activates your body's metabolism, so that calories are continuously burnt off, which means that you will feel less hungry at mealtimes and therefore eat less.

However, not everyone agrees with this argument. An interesting experiment was carried out in 2012 by Mitsutoshi Hatori, a researcher at the University of Tokyo. Two groups of mice were fed with the same amount of food over a period of 100 days. The first group was free to eat the food at any time of day or night. The second group was given their food at specific times each day. At the end of the experiment, the mice that could eat according to their will weighed 30% more than the mice that ate according to a fixed schedule. In addition, the mice in the second group displayed a number of other positive dietary effects, such as lower inflammation values, greater glucose tolerance, better liver functioning and superior motor skills.

I am strongly against eating snacks between meals and am sure that people who follow my guidance will nearly all be able to lose weight sustainably.

CONCRETE NUTRITIONAL ADVICE

After I have explained the relationship between sugars and insulin secretion, the vast majority of my coachees have little difficulty following my fundamental nutritional advice. Avoid simple sugars as far as possible, and certainly between meals. Limit yourself to three meals each day (to avoid intermediary insulin spikes). Ensure a snack-free period of 12 to 13 hours in every 24-hour cycle, preferably between your evening meal and the next morning's breakfast (which also means taking your evening meal early). Last but not least, stop eating before you feel full.

Sticking to these guidelines leads to a sustainable loss of weight in nearly all my coachees, often without the need to give extra advice about what they should and shouldn't eat. The strict avoidance of simple sugars alone is generally a guarantee for success. For the rest, bringing structure to your eating habits is more important than what you actually eat.

Avoid simple sugars and restrict yourself
to three eating moments per day.

Don't play yo-yo

People who are overweight often try to correct the situation by following a low-calorie diet, based on advice from nutritional experts who tell them to scrupulously avoid fats or carbohydrates. This kind of diet usually works up to a point. The excess kilograms disappear rapidly. But within months, the dieters are again overweight and have even added a few kilos extra. This is the so-called yo-yo effect.

The reason for this is simple to understand. Diets of this kind are essentially punishment diets. Every day, you consume fewer calories than you burn (a negative calorie balance), which means that you are constantly denying yourself things that you like. But you can only keep this up for a limited period. After a time, you start to notice that you are losing less and less weight, even though you are maintaining the same level of effort.

In other words, your body has become used to your low-calorie regime and has adjusted by slowing down your metabolic rate. In short, it can manage on less energy, burning less fat. As a result, your energy loss stabilises. If you want to get your weight down even more, you can only do so by making an even greater dietary effort.

This can be discouraging and in many cases people just fall back into their old 'high energy' eating habits after a couple of months, but now with a lower rate of fat burning. This means that not only do your lost kilos return in no time, but your weight will probably continue to climb above its original level. To make matters worse, this reduced metabolic rate, once created, can sometimes be permanent. Which is a very good reason for steering clear of all radical crash-diets that seem so popular.

Don't make yourself fat!

'*Maak je niet dik*' (literally meaning 'Don't make yourself fat') is an old Flemish saying used in response to people who are upset about something. Physiolog-ically, the saying makes sense, because when you are upset the body secretes the stress hormone cortisol into your blood.

One effect of cortisol is increased blood sugar levels. This is an understandable natural reaction by your body, since extra sugar gives you the extra energy you need to deal with the stressful situation. Once this situation is resolved, your blood sugar level returns to normal. But what if the stress situation persists, so that your sugar level remains high? This will also increase your insulin level, so that more and more fat is stored in your cells. Conclusion: continuous stress literally makes you fat.

But it doesn't end there. If you're stressed, free radicals are also released into your body. These are minute chemical entities, which occur as a normal part of the metabolic process and bind to your cells. As long as the number of free radicals remains within bounds, there is no problem. But if circumstances arise that increase their number beyond acceptable limits, they can become aggres-sive and risk causing serious harm to your health. In particular, they lower your body's natural resistance. This not only increases your susceptibility to illness and infection, but also your likelihood of being affected by cancer and heart complaints, as well as accelerating the ageing process and further reducing your stress tolerance. Factors that can lead to an increase in the number of free radicals include air pollution, ageing, tiredness, excessive physical effort, continuous stress…

By increasing the content of anti-oxidants in your diet, it is possible to counteract the negative impact of free radicals. One such powerful anti-oxidant is vitamin C, which can be found in vegetables, citrus fruits, potatoes, berries and strawberries. Vitamin E is also effective and occurs in vegetables, fruit, nuts, sunflower oil, diet margarine, bread and cereal products.

Sleep yourself thin

Your pattern of sleep also has a key influence on your weight control. Poor sleep is a contributor to both weight gain and the likelihood of diabetes. Once again, the reason is simple. Lack of sleep increases stress and in turn the release of cortisol into the bloodstream. From then on, it's the familiar story: glucose levels rise, additional insulin is secreted to combat it and more fat is stored in your cells...

Your amount of sleep also impacts two other important hormones: ghrelin and leptin. Ghrelin is the hormone that improves your appetite, while leptin has the precise opposite effect. A lack of sleep has been shown to increase the natural production of ghrelin and reduce the production of leptin. As a result, sleep deprivation gives you a much greater feeling of hunger.

It's clear that controlling your weight is a complex matter that demands an all-inclusive approach. A straightforward analysis of what you eat and simply limiting your calorie intake will not achieve the results you hope for; in fact, quite the reverse. Nutritional experts really need to become health coaches, who adopt a multi-disciplinary perspective with their patients, offering advice not only about food but also about exercise and sleep.

Shortage of sleep
makes you eat.

Jan cut back his number of daily coffees to just three, the last of which he drank around midday. He also stopped eating all sweet things. Before long, he was feeling the positive effects, in terms of greater energy and alertness. 'It's strange,' he said to me. 'I'm drinking much less coffee than I used to, but I never seem to yawn anymore during the day!'

Tips

» Avoid simple sugars (sweets, cakes, biscuits, chocolate, soft drinks).

» Opt for fibre-rich carbohydrates (brown bread, wholemeal bread, wholemeal breakfast cereals, wholemeal pasta and brown rice).

» Eat three pieces of fruit every day, but avoid (freshly pressed) fruit juice.

» Eat at three fixed times each day.

» Avoid snacks between your three meals.

» Never follow a crash diet.

» Make sure you get a good night's rest.

Conclusion

Nowadays, lots of people feel 'stuck'. Many of us have a vague realisation that we need to do things differently, but they don't always take the necessary action. Even knowing this, it's still extremely difficult to convince people to make the change as they're unable to place what they do and feel in a broader context – in the big picture. And yet this picture is the one that sticks by us for the rest of our lives.

To help, I nearly always confront my coachees with the following graphic, asking them which of the three lines they want to choose.

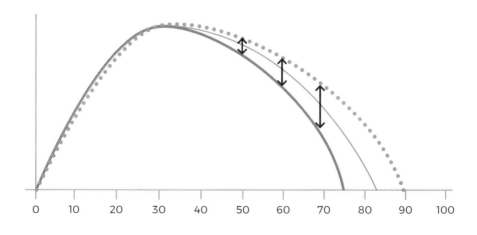

THE POSSIBLE IMPACT OF LIFESTYLE ON QUALITY OF LIFE

The blue line shows the 'normal' course of your life, in terms of quality and longevity. Average life expectancy is currently just over 80 years. You are at your strongest around your 30th birthday. After that, you enter a process of irreversible physical decline – hardly noticeable at first but increasingly evident until the day that it takes way longer to recover from strenuous physical activity and even from a night out on the town.

But we don't all go downhill at the same rate. Some of us continue performing at higher levels for longer than others and it's the result of numerous factors – most notably our genes. But don't lose hope! A lot is in our control. The extent to which we take good care of ourselves is often decisive of our overall health and well-being in the long run.

The black line in the graph on the previous page shows the likely progress of our lives if we don't take care of ourselves, if we don't make time for ourselves, if we don't get enough sleep, if we don't eat healthily… We are constantly fighting our weight, drinking too much alcohol, exercising too little, sitting too much for long and unbroken periods, with too much stress. We often underestimate the impact of these factors on the quality and length of our lives – putting us only in peril.

In contrast, the dotted line shows the likely outcome of our lives as true Egopreneurs. If we look after ourselves adequately, if we take accountability for the crucial factors that make us physically and mentally stronger, that bring us greater mental resilience – then we're on the right track.

You can see that the difference between the blue line and the broken line starts out small. But as time takes its toll, the distance quickly increases, starting to reflect our quality of life.

This diagram and its explanations have raised quite some coachees' eyebrows over the years. But the wisdom in following the dotted line was painfully clear. How could they do otherwise? It's simply a question of logic. But I quickly confessed that while it might be the best and most logical choice, it's by no means the easiest. It demands commitment and a lot of hard work.

SO WHICH LINE DO YOU CHOOSE?

I hope that you opt resolutely for the dotted line and that you're prepared for the effort that comes with it. Use this book as your guide in a trajectory that will not only allow you to strengthen yourself, but also to become more able to help others. You can do it! Make time for yourself, sleep at least seven hours each night, exercise every day, limit your consumption of alcohol, avoid simple sugars and keep a close watch on your weight. This will take you a long way towards your goal.

SO WHAT ARE YOU WAITING FOR? COMMIT TO THE DOTTED LINE AND GROW INTO YOUR BEST SELF – INTO AN EGOPRENEUR.